SOLOMON'S WAY

THE ANCIENT SECRETS AND METHODS OF A SEDUCER

Christopher J. Solomon

Copyright 2015 by Christopher J. Solomon
The book author retains sole copyright to
his contributions to this book.

Published 2015.
Printed in the United States of America.

All rights reserved. No portion of this book may
be reproduced, stored in a retrieval system, or
transmitted in any form or by any means –
electronic, mechanical, photocopy, recording,
scanning, or other – except for brief quotations
in critical reviews or articles, without the prior
written permission of the author.

ISBN 978-1-937862-85-5

Library of Congress Control Number 2015907229

This book was published by BookCrafters,
Parker, Colorado.
bookcrafters@comcast.net

This book may be ordered from
www.bookcrafters.net
and other online bookstores.

DEDICATION

TO MOM

TO DAD

TO ALL WOMEN

ACKNOWLEDGEMENTS

The following are a few Seducers of their own fields who I call friends: Laos, Vu, LT, Big Pun, Pitt Bull, OSO, Scooby, Lucky, Phi, Brian, Tiempo, Goo, Head, Nguyen, Tony, Jeff, Hi, Kingpin.

My Sifu who is a Master Seducer, Shaolin High Priest Ricky E. Anderson.

My Eternal Loves Cherie, Aimee and Dirty Baby.

My Special Loves Corina, Rainbow and Stephanie.

CONTENTS

Foreword
1. The World and Your Understanding.....................1
2. The Problem..12
3. The Solution...20
4. The Method..29
5. The Application..37
6. The Excuses...46
7. The Answers..53
8. The Headaches..64
9. The 9 Fundamental Characteristics of A True Seducer..69
10. The Sexual Power of Names............................72
11. The World Through Her Eyes -
    The Secrets Of Eye Contact............................80
12. The Secrets of Observation............................86
13. Women Through the Ages..............................93
14. The Secrets of Silence....................................99
15. Her Inner Sex Goddess Unleashed
    (H.I.S. Goddess)..104
16. The Secret Life of a Seducer........................108

FOREWORD

Of the many books that are found on bookshelves in bookstores everywhere, there exists a section dedicated to the themes of dating, seduction and sex and combinations of the three in different orders of magnitude. This section exists for those who find the opposite sex, not only worthy of study, but also difficult and hard to figure out, like trying to find one's way through the woods blindfolded in the dark of the night.

Having read many of these beautifully bound books, some of which contained good techniques and good ideas for the common man to explore, I found that most of them only concentrated on personality and various methods of how to best display charm, wit and humor. That literature was thoughtfully entertaining at best, but it did not even begin to skim the surface of Seduction the way I had hoped.

For the past 18 years, I have studied many of these tomes, not because I needed them, but because I was interested in what they had to say. They were, after all, discussing my favorite subject in the world: WOMEN. Sifting through the pounds and pounds of literature, I found many things that were noteworthy, many points to ponder and keep in mind, and even some things that were written, obviously, for the sole purpose of gaining a laugh.

My eyes could not believe some of the tactics many of these pick-up artists deployed. Of course, if that is what works for them, then I applaud their achievements. But I read these books these very entertaining books dedicated to what I love most, not to gain wisdom from them.

Quite the contrary, I read these books to see if any of them had described in picture perfect clarity the Ancient Secrets and Methods of Seduction. I was curious to see if they knew what I know. I wanted to see if they were, indeed, Seducers. And as it stands, they did not, they do not, and they are not. So, after taking note of man's inability to see clearly, I have decided to lay bare the The Ancient Secrets and Methods of Seduction.

In this great work, you will not find what has already been printed in books elsewhere. You will not find steps to follow, affirmations, clothes to wear or extreme personality make-overs. In this work, what you will find is hardcore truth, undefiled wisdom, and a primal understanding that will not only change, but also enhance your sexual success with women forever.

Once you absorb this knowledge and wisdom, you will wonder how you ever did without it. But beware, this is not for everyone. Once your eyes have been opened, there will be no closing them.

Christopher J. Solomon
January 15, 2015

Women are women.
Not men.

Women have not changed since
the dawn of time and they won't.

Men are designed to be with women a
nd women are designed to enjoy it.

Women can enjoy
crossing the finish line
over and over again.

1

THE WORLD AND YOUR UNDERSTANDING

e all have different eyes through which we see the world. We all have our filters, multicolored lenses that define the vast landscapes before us. What is a beautiful snow-capped mountain to one is but a grotesque mound of dirt with bird droppings on top to another. The way one person sees the world will never be exactly the same as someone else sees it no matter how hard we try to convince them or ourselves otherwise.

The way men see women suffers the same fate. Everyone has their own telescopic view of what a woman is or what a woman should be. One man may see a grade school teacher whose days of driving the opposite sex wild with lust has long passed. Another may see a mother whose only concern at present is the care and nurturing of her off spring. And yet, still another may see a district court judge who is the personification of justice, law and all that is right. And beyond all of these titles they are also aunts, grandmothers, sisters and daughters. This is as true as the sky is blue, but there is a common thread that is often over-looked often ignored, or just plain disregarded. And that is the fact that they are all women.

Women all possess the same structure. They all have the same amount of bones within their bodies. They all possess more curves than a man. Their features are softer, their voices are higher pitched, their skin more receptive and appreciative of tender caresses. But there is yet an even deeper commonality that lurks beneath such an enticing exterior. They all possess the same brain structure.

Deep within the recesses of the female brain, just beyond the darkest part of the woods over the river, next to the castle, lies a place that is extremely receptive to sexual pleasure. And that place, like a glowing ball of lightning has its tentacles spread throughout the entire structure of a woman's being, ready and waiting for the slightest hint of sexual stimulation whether it is physical, mental or emotional or all the above. This is not make-believe, this is biology.

Such scientific thinking seems far too simplistic, the common man seems to say. And while divorcing himself from such thoughts, everything else started to get in the way. He has to get up early for work in the morning. He has problems he has to solve before Friday. He also has to pay for the utilities before they turn off his electricity. All these distractions blind men from seeing what's before them. Their focus becomes fixed on the first shiny object that appears thus their attention is directed elsewhere.

Suddenly, they are too tired, too busy, too distracted.

SOLOMON'S WAY

There are other things of more importance. And then the urge hits them. They want a woman, but they don't know the first thing to do in their pursuit. What was a simple line has now become a mass of circles. And so men retreat in defeat. But if men hope to succeed with women, they must wake from this trance and live not as a troll under the bridge, but as the barbarian with a bevy of beauties at his side.

Women have not changed since the dawn of time and they won't. They still love us men and desire us in much the same way that we do them. But women nowadays are afraid to show it because at some point in your travels, you allowed less important things become more important than her. It is as if you failed to realize a very important truth of our species. You failed to understand that men are designed to be with womenand women are designed to enjoy it. Based on this understanding alone your sexual success will increase exponentially.

Women are sad though because very few men understand. They are sad that you just don't get it. You would rather stand in your own way. You start to bring your moods, your likes, your dislikes, your feelings to the playground. And so she retreats because she feels you are behaving strangely. She no longer wants to play with you or allow you to play with her.

When you become your own Seduction, you only end up with yourself. She just wants to know that you can take care of her pleasure. Understand that women do not care about what you have going on with you. It's that simple. Women are selfish creatures like that. And that is quite all right.

Women are designed to enjoy sex about a million times more powerfully than a man. This may seem hard to believe at first, but it is true. All women have a special feature about their beautiful bodies, a feature that men seem to overlook when casting a quick glance at a woman.

Women possess an organ that serves no other biological function than that of producing extreme amounts of sexual pleasure. This organ, sometimes referred to as a button is the clitoris.

The clitoris, or button, has the power to drive women insane with sexual pleasure. An active volcano doesn't even begin to burn half as bright as that of a woman whose clitoris has been stimulated. It can propel them from the darkest depths of the ocean to the crater surface of the moon at the blink of an eye.

Combine this button and the power it beholds with the sensitive nerve endings present at the opening of the vagina and you have that ball of lightning deep within the recesses of her brain surging with the force of a thousand suns.

But this isn't all. Sure, the charging is fun and women enjoy it lovingly but what they truly enjoy is the discharge of all this energy. And this discharge, this releasing of all pent up energy is what women know and love as the orgasm. The orgasm is the cherry on top of all that whipped cream. The crowning jewel. The finish line. And another secret of women is they can experience crossing this finish line over and over again, back to back, multiple times, like a song stuck on repeat.

And finally to conclude the basic structure of women, there are also many different types of orgasms a woman may experience. A woman's orgasms may be vaginal, clitoral, anal, bodily, all of the above or varying magnitudes of only a few. All of the different species of orgasms share the common trait of taking her into the land of orgasms or simply Orgasmland.

Orgasmland is the place where all of a woman's sexual pleasure peaks, taking her into sweet sexual overload. Her body shakes, quivers and crumbles into submission as she reaches fulfillment. Women who have never been to Orgasmland inherently know that this beautiful place exists simply because the long and windy roads leading there are so beautiful.

For the women who have been there, they soon discover that Orgasmland is a place they never want to leave. It becomes a place they always want to return to, no matter the weather. But all of this knowledge is meant to be a secret. This kind of information is not for everyone. It's meant for those who truly understand women and what they want.

It is because of this naked truth that she must show she has morals. She must show restraint, discretion and a facade that is totally opposite to that of her true nature. It's a must lest they render themselves to quivering masses of goo.

A good face must be put on and costumes must be worn so only Seducers know what's going on while the rest of the world goes about their daily business none the wiser, the costumes having done their jobs misdirecting a mass audience.

This magnificent display of self-control by nearly all women causes something even more unique to happen. In not being able to fulfill their desires and return to Orgasmland as much as they would like to, the need to return there becomes more magnified. The need becomes so great that this lightning ball of energy deep within her brain, that is extremely receptive to sexual pleasure, begins to amplify the receptivity of the tentacles embedded throughout the entire structure of women.

What this means is her mind drools at the mouth ready to associate anything that comes through the channels of her eyes, ears, touch and/or thoughts with something sexual. She is desperate to return to Orgasmland. It's a must for her well-being.

Her imagination begins to visualize dirty things all throughout the day, but society would have you believe that it is only men who think more about sex, not women. The late great psychoanalyst, Dr. Sigmund Freud, said it best when he said, "If men knew how women really thought, they would be ten-times more bold." The doctor knew a thing or two about women.

So, women crave and seek out sex in places where it does not exist because they are in dire need of pleasure. That is how women are designed.

Since women get to wear costumes to hide the burning within, they also like to see things such as their own personal play or movie or, better yet, soap opera. Of course, it's difficult as a man, to grasp this concept, but you must.

Women don't see the world the way we do. When we interact with women, we usually do so with an end result in mind. Women, on the other hand, not only see the end result, their desire to return to Orgasmland, they also revel in the journey there.

Women see every interaction with men as a scene from a play, and every subsequent interaction as a different scene in that same play. Sure, she make things lovey dovey and romantic, but within all of the different scenes, she hopes you will hoist her over your shoulder and take her to the bedroom on her way to Orgasmland. You are, after all, not only the audience but also the lead male character. It is written in the script that you be the one to pleasure her. Subdue her primary biological desires.

Now that you can begin to understand the basic structure of women, we shall discuss the way a woman's world works.

As men, we are designed to be very literal, very concrete, problem solvers, egotistical. That's just the way we men are designed. There is absolutely nothing wrong with that. Just understand that women do not share our brains. They are not men. They are women. They do not take in the world the way we do.

Women care about relationships, communication, beauty, soft, sweet and cute things. Things we really don't care about. But the point is we don't have to care about these things because this is what is in a woman's world. What this basically means is the things you care about at that particular moment are not going to be the same things she cares about that same moment. Unless, of course, you care about taking her to Orgasmland, then, you would be on the same page.

A woman expects a man to be strong, forceful, decisive and manly. And in being all of these things, she also expects a man to be able to take care of her sexual pleasure and protect her. These last two things are the basic duties of a man. She should know that when she is with you, she will not be harmed by anyone and that at a moment's notice, you would peel her clothes off with your teeth.

It is a concept that many men find hard to believe, but it is possible to have a relationship with a woman or women based on nothing more than the pursuit of sexual pleasure. Nothing more. Details about the day, work, the family, etc. play no part in this relationship. There need not be any common ground beyond the fact that you are a man and she is a woman. Everything else just gets in the way.

Of course, it is usually men who place distractions in the way of the main objective which is her sexual pleasure and the pursuit of it. How can a man begin to protect a woman he's afraid to talk to? How will he be able to provide her with sexual pleasure if he's afraid to get near her?

Somewhere along the way, man began to see all the flaws within himself. And since he could see these flaws so clearly, he figured, surely a woman will be able to see them clearly also. So, man began to carry this belief with him everywhere until his focus and attention were no longer on her. Now they were on him. You must always remember that it is never about you. It is about her.

By pleasing a woman, you will in turn be pleased. That is the way it works. Seducing yourself is no Seduction at all. Seeing yourself as some ladies' man is not something she particularly cares about or finds as interesting as you. The man whose focus is on the woman and not on himself is the man who will be successful in his pursuits.

Do not focus on how you're coming across, how you think you sound, or how you look. All of these things are in perfect proportion because you are a man. Period. She should always be the focus of your attention. She's on stage. It's her theater. You are the audience and the lead male character. Shut up and let her do her dance.

Men foolishly believe that if we are big, bad and awesome to our guy friends, women will see us in

SOLOMON'S WAY

the same light. This is a flawed thinking. Women are not men and do not see things as we do. Sure, you're cool among the men, but you look like an idiot to women. And who matters most? Definitely not your buddies.

The coolest guy in the world is that guy who has his choice of women. It doesn't matter what he looks like, how much money he has, what clothes he wears. Those things don't matter because with his choice of women, he has the potential to inherit the world!

Many men falsely believe that it is, the other way around: get money, get clothes, a car, a nice home, then get women. This is wrong. Any woman who needs these things in a man before she'll have sex with him is a user, and things will more than likely end ugly. Remember, men have been bedding women for a very long time. Cave men had nothing more than the hair that covered their bodies. And nothing has changed in women. It is that simple. Nothing is needed that you don't already possess. You being a man is enough.

Of course, this all sounds far-fetched and too good to be true. Some people would rather have steps to follow, like all it takes is following these three steps.. Steps are unnecessary. Knowledge and wisdom of women is what's most important of all.

Perhaps an illustration is in order. Take for example, the latest cellular phone and its different versions. There is a certain circuitry that is common to all phones. It could be something as simple as the way a phone uses energy from the battery. It doesn't matter what make or model the phone is. The way the phone uses the energy from the battery is common to all phones. If you know this basic bit of simple circuitry, you know all phones.

The same goes for women. If you know basic bits of their circuitry, you know women. And having this wisdom is what it is all about. Your skin color, job, education, money, mean absolutely nothing. All you have to be is male and human. And everything else is secondary.

𝕾𝖚𝖇𝖉𝖚𝖊 𝖍𝖊𝖗 𝖕𝖗𝖎𝖒𝖆𝖗𝖞
𝖇𝖎𝖔𝖑𝖔𝖌𝖎𝖈𝖆𝖑 𝖉𝖊𝖘𝖎𝖗𝖊𝖘.

2

THE PROBLEM

Women are frustrated. Men don't seem to get the signals sent their way. We're always too busy wrapped up in our own world. We mistakenly think we can think what women think, but the truth is we cannot. We, therefore, miss 99% of what's said to us. Women do not like this at all. They begin to feel ignored despite the words they say.

The problem is men need to open their eyes and see through new rose-colored lenses. It is not their fault you don't understand what they are telling you. Women don't want to have to explain it to you. You're supposed to do your homework and know what women mean. You must put forth a tiny bit of effort.

If you recognize how a woman's mind works, you'll begin to see women for what they really are: restrained Sex Goddesses. As stated earlier, a woman's mind will go sexual any chance it gets. As a mature woman, she is very aware of this. And as a result, there begins to exist an anticipation. Her mind begins to naturally seek it out, those tentacles of that lightning ball in her brain surging with energy.

She seeks not only words, but actions, gestures and thoughts placed before her that imply something sexual. Therefore, something as innocent as "it's harder than you think," leaves room for misinterpretation. A woman's first and foremost thought is sexual. But only she knows it. This allows her to cherish the moment and then, quickly, change the subject before anyone can read her thoughts.

Women speak a language that men can't seem to hear. It's specifically designed to bypass and weed out those who aren't tuned in to the frequencies of her biological desire. Only those tuned-in know that a woman doesn't always say she means and what she means isn't always what she says. Women speak more of what they feel in their body than what they think in their head.

But a woman can't really voice what she desires lest she be called a disrespectful name. So, the feeling remains in her body while her words allude to something totally opposite in subject matter. Then, it becomes two languages embedded in one.

One language travels on a high frequency which contains trivial subject matter and the other language travels on a lower frequency. This lower frequency language speaks directly of a woman's biological desire. This lower language is the one you should be tuned-in to.

Men who can tune in to this biological frequency will be miles ahead of anyone else in competition. You will not be misled by words, distracted or thrown off the scent. You will know how to listen to what she's really saying.

One must never assume that just because a woman talks to him that he speaks the same language that she does or that she is interested in him in that way. Words can easily betray, and he could just be a cure for her boredom until someone comes along who speaks her language.

A woman judges a potential partner very quickly. What this means for you is you must show her that you can speak her language before she dismisses you as a common man.

Women want to be loved, cherished and adored, but they also want to unleash that Inner Sex Goddess who, not only can please men, but also takes pleasure and pride in it.

Women love that they can orgasm until they literally run out of energy. They love being drained, feeling sore, being out of breath and cotton-mouthed due to sex. It is true. But the problem is, men seem to either forget this truth or they don't know this truth.

It is sad state for men because nothing can change many years of biological response. But for some reason or another, men think women are foreign to us. Men believe women are hard to understand, difficult to be around or talk to.

Men complicate things. Women are just women. There is no reason to fear them. A man doesn't fear walking alone at night down the street because there is a group women lurking in the dark. But put a woman in that situation with a group of men out there . . . You see my point.

Women are our softer, sweeter, feminine counterparts. They want us to win them because they love us and they want to be won. But understand, through all the sweetness, all the softness, all the things she may say she likes, what she's into, how she dresses like, all of this is secondary to her biology as a woman. She is a goddess waiting to be unleashed and every man has that key to release her.

But men like to play games with themselves and pretend they no longer hold the key. They go about trying to find the key. They search high and low, even change things about themselves because they figure it will make them irresistible to women. Drastic changes will only have the opposite effect.

Women don't care about what you have, how you see yourself, or even what you look like. Women are selfish and they really just want to know if you can take care of their biological desire.

Once she senses your doubt in this area, she will begin to have doubts. And suddenly, you're trying to talk your way out of a freshly dug grave. You're trying to convince her that you can take care of her biological desire. Although it is possible to recover, it is difficult and it takes time. All this could have been avoided if you had sent the right signals in the first place. And the way to send the right signals is through confidence.

Confidence has been thrown around for a long time and with good reason. She can't begin to feel comfortable around you if you don't feel comfortable with yourself around her. How can she let her hair down if you're feeling up-tight and shaky just because she is present? Any kind of self-doubt that you feel within yourself is immediately picked up by women.

Women are experts on reading emotions. You make the situation weird by feeling weird which makes her feel uncomfortable. Women want to feel secure in your presence, but that only comes with being secure in yourself.

Remember women expect men to be men. This means that when a woman comes near a man, she expect to be the main focus of his attention. She expects to talk, be cherished and adored. She expects to feel more like a woman in the presence of a man and she in turn makes a man feel more like a man. This is how our species work.

A man must make a woman the center of his universe for a time. This does not mean being loud and stupid. That impresses males, not females. What impresses females is being attentive, listening and paying attention to what she says on the lower frequency. Your focus should be on her, not on yourself.

The things women love are things men find too girly, too soft, too pink. Men think that since we, as men don't like girly stuff that women won't like them either. As ridiculous as this sounds, this is how men think. It is tragic. And because of this flawed thinking, men begin to say and do things that they enjoy, such as being loud, cracking jokes, teasing and being crass. Sure there may be a few women who do enjoy such behavior, but they are hard to find.

Don't believe that such behavior will lead to satisfying a woman's biological need. It will not.

You cannot use the same language you use with your male friends with females. They hear something totally different. They speak totally different. They are totally different.

Men speak one language and it's primarily used for the sole purpose of giving information. Women, on the other hand, speak one other language in addition to the two mentioned earlier. Women speak the visual language, body language.

There is a lot that goes on in a woman's world. We

SOLOMON'S WAY

can only understand so much, but we'll be better equipped knowing of the language differences. We don't have to completely enter a woman's world to understand it. All we need to know is how they see things. This doesn't mean seeing through their eyes. This simply means processing knowledge of how they see things. The man who believes he must completely enter a woman's world, i.e. like what she likes, what she feels, is doomed to be nothing more than a friend to women forever.

This is the man who believes he is gaining points and is on his way into her bedroom. Nothing can be further from the truth. This is the guy she'll complain to about the guy who treated her badly, who had sex with her and didn't call, the guy who tried to put things where they didn't belong.

And because of this "friend" gets to hear all of this, he thinks he has won somehow. Why else would she be telling me these things? he thinks to himself not realizing that the guy who really won is the guy she's complaining about.

This poor sap also doesn't realize that she's really not complaining, but using the medium of complaining as reason enough to talk about that man with another man.

You must never let a woman discuss another man with you. The more she talks about him, the more he's on her mind, not you. When she tells the same so-called complaints to her girlfriends, you can believe her tone will be a softer, more seductive tone, and all details will be discussed, details edited out with you.

She will praise him, adore him, be so happy that he did what he did because it is what made her feel more like a woman. And it also makes her girlfriends jealous. It is these things women love most. Don't be fooled by the angelic faces of our women. They are the world's best actresses and the world is their stage.

SOLOMON'S WAY

She expects you to be strong,
forceful, decisive and manly.

Everything else
just gets in the way.

3

THE SOLUTION

Now that we have identified the problem and opened your eyes to the world around you, perhaps you can begin to see the solution. That solution is you.

The parallels between the problem and the solution should be evident. You and your understanding of the world, women and how they operate, and your lack of knowing such things was the problem. Now the solution which is you and your unique understanding of the above will empower your pursuits as you now possess the ability to see how things really are.

First, upon encountering a woman to whom you are sexually attracted, your first sight is to see her as a woman. Uniforms, make-up, job titles, age, race, financial and educational background mean absolutely nothing. These are all potential distractions and are secondary to her primary function as a woman. Understanding this may seem too simplistic and that's only because it is.

SOLOMON'S WAY

It is all too simple, but we feel that if something is too simple it can't be right, can't be correct, can't be so. And so we devise ways to complicate things until a simple straight line from point A to point B becomes an entire chalkboard full of circles, triangles, hearts, stars and horseshoes. Sounds crazy, doesn't it? Women seem to think so, too.

Let's say that you have spotted a woman who is very appealing to you. Who she is, what she is, where she's from doesn't matter. All that is important at present is that she is a woman. What does this mean? This means that since she is a woman, she has circuitry that is biological in nature. It is nothing she can over-ride. It's embedded in her design and therefore, in every fiber of her being.

Remember, women all have a sexual pleasure button. The sole purpose of this button is to bring sexual pleasure to every woman. This button is the woman's friend because it brings her wonderful, earth shattering orgasms.

A woman longs to unleash her Inner Sex Goddess, to be broken free of her bonds and social restraints. This is the dark and very real under-current running through every woman's being.

So, at every instance, anytime, anything is said or done that could possibly unleash the Goddess from within her and make her fantasy a reality, her mind is on it, ready and willing to make it a reality. Keep this at the forefront of your mind and you'll see things from the height of a throne.

You will be tuned into her in a way very few men are. This shows that you're not selfish, and if it's one thing women hate, it's a selfish lover.

You must be able to take control of your interactions

with women. If women sense that you are weak, afraid, and unable to stand your ground around women, they will not see you as a strong, powerful, sexual man who can take care of their needs sexually. They will see you as a man they can control, dominate and make eat out of their hands.

The woman will call the shots in these cases. Nothing prosperous comes from that kind of relationship. Only disgust and pity sex, if there is any sex at all. Most men would be happy with this kind of relationship, but you should not be. This is not what nature intended for man.

In order for her to see you as a strong, powerful and sexual man, you must project a certain kind of confidence, a sexual confidence. This is a confidence that says you can provide her with sexual pleasure and protect her from harm. It's as simple as that.

You have to believe that with every fiber of your being you can take care of these two most basic needs. If you falter in this belief, she will sense it and all will be lost.

It should be noted that there was no mention of appearance, money or belongings. The reason for this is because those things are secondary. They don't matter as much as people would have you believe.

Cave men, which weren't attractive to the eye by anyone's standards, which didn't possess money or belongings, were able to breed with their choice of females. Why? Because they were able to provide pleasure and they were able to protect. Nothing else mattered. This can be true for you today, if you truly want it.

It is difficult for many men to wrap their head around the idea that a man can have relationships with women based on nothing more than sex. It is true, but what might be even harder to believe is that the sexual relationship was the very first kind of relationship men had with women.

It was and still is instinctual. Men and women came together because they both fulfilled each other sexually, which in turn meant the continuation of their genes. Later on, as men created more things, he became more distracted and began to take his focus off women and the primary relationship he had with her. But biology hasn't changed in women or men.

Everything that was present in cave men and cave women is still present today in modern day men and women. All you have to do is look within yourself and reclaim what is rightfully yours: WOMEN.

There is no limit to the number of women you can have sexual relationships with. Only you can say how many is enough. It was no uncommon for a man to have 700 wives and 300 concubines in some societies. This is your right as a man.

Focus, not on yourself but on women. They shall be your focus. Once you devote your attention to women with the knowledge you now possess and the unshakable confidence to protect and provide, you shall inherit all the women you can fulfill. This is how nature intended it. Understand that it is not about you or what you think. It is all about what you can do for her.

The most important thing a woman thinks is, "Can you take care of my sexual pleasure?" If you can take care of this, she'll automatically feel protected. Why? Because unless she feels safe, she won't have sex with you.

Women are smarter than you would give them credit. Their vision, hearing, intuition and language are far superior to ours. They can play chess, but not with ordinary pieces. No, they prefer to use humans, relationships and emotions. And if you're not careful, you may become just a pawn in her wicked game.

Many men have fallen victim, unknowingly, because they were not aware of the knowledge that you are now aware.

Women will have you believe that you have to take them out to eat, buy them things, drive a Mercedes, own a mansion, have a big bank account and be something like a CEO at your place of employment. These are all things she would like you to have because Ken and Barbie had them, but you don't have to have them.

Your existence as a man and your ability to pleasure her is all that you need. It has worked this way for thousands of years and will continue to do so for as long as humans exist.

Once in the presence of a woman or women, you must project masculinity and confidence. Women must always be aware of the fact that you are a man, but not just any man, who will accept bratty behavior. No, you must be that man who makes a woman feel more like a woman. That's the man who constantly makes a woman aware of her femininity. The one who constantly reminds her, non-verbally, that he would fulfill her biological desire at the drop of a hat. This is the kind of man that women swoon over. This is the kind of man women wish men would be.

She will never mistake him for a weakling because of the raw sexual power he presents to her. She will always know that when she is in his presence, the costumes and fancy titles mean nothing. She is to him only a woman. And this is how it should be. She must never lose sight of this.

She should be reminded that she can be sexually

pleased right there, right now and that the rest of the world doesn't exist. And all that matters is her and her pleasure.

You must convey through your presence the raw primal desire to fulfill her needs, you don't care where she is from, who her friends are, where she works, or any other nonsense like that. Show her nothing matters but your desire for her, and that the most important thing to you is her and her pleasure.

Women can easily read these signals because they are basic to their being. They are the most primal of signals. And once she reads them, it will begin to awaken a part of her that's been long asleep. She'll begin to feel that Goddess within her twitching for release.

You may begin to notice changes about her. Her breathing may become deeper, she'll break eye-contact and look back at you with soft eyes. Her body may squirm or a combination of all of the above.

When a woman feels something, anything, when it comes to emotions, this feeling is not centrally located in one spot. She feels this feeling throughout her body. So, she may begin to fidget, move around, giggle, or even turn to walk away. She really doesn't want to leave, but there's a lot going on in her body and in her mind that made her excited. She enjoys this feeling and slowly her Inner Goddess prepares for release.

It must be understood that you do not stand around like a psych patient, linger like a lost child, or show desperation like an obsessed fan. Your demeanor must be cool, calm and collected. Your desire should be evident, not through inappropriate physical arousal, but through your energy.

Your entire being should radiate with this primal

energy. Your movements shall not be hurried, insecure or animated. A lion does not have to bare his fangs to a gazelle in order for the gazelle to know it can and will be eaten at a moment's notice. And so it is with women. They know instinctively that they can be had for lunch.

Women easily pick up on the subtle cues in your demeanor. Again, this is how they are hot-wired. It's part of their circuitry. If you come across as weird or peculiar, any chance you may have thought you had before will be lost.

Instead, you will trigger the other side of her circuitry, the part that seeks safety. A woman only seeks safety in the presence of a man she considers a threat. Not a potential lover.

Women are much like cats in the way that they don't show their need for affection the way dogs do. Be not mistaken, though. They very much need affection. They just have a very unique way of showing it. You must press, but not too hard and not too overtly. Like cats, they'll come around.

Remember, when it comes to a man and a woman, it is not supposed to be a public affair. It is supposed to be between the man and woman. Your friends have no say so. Her friends have no say so. Don't be a fool and believe that her friends or your friends are more important than what you have going on with her. Nothing is above you and her.

Your male friends and your playful banter with them will not make a woman swoon over you, although this is a common belief among men. Men oftentimes use their friends as crutches or a safety net when it comes to talking to a woman. This is because a man's friends give him courage and confidence where it is lacking, and if a negative response from a woman is levied his way,

SOLOMON'S WAY

the impact on his ego is reduced because it's equally distributed amongst him and friends. But falling back on friends is fear based. You must eliminate such fear.

Women are just women and are naturally more afraid of men than men are of them. It's funny how men can hunt, fight wars, cause the utmost destruction upon the earth, yet fear creatures so soft and feminine as women. It makes no sense. It is time men stop being fearful of women. It is time men start being men.

CHRISTOPHER J. SOLOMON

By pleasing a woman,
you will in turn be pleased.
Women don't want to have to spell
it out for you.

4

THE METHOD

Long before the invention of language, cars, clothes, homes and the modern world as we know it, there existed a unique and subtle way of attracting the opposite sex. This method still persists today, but not everyone is aware or keen to this Ancient method. This Ancient method is called "the Copulatory Gaze."

The Copulatory Gaze is the oldest and most Ancient mating signal of the human species. It transcends all language, racial, economic and educational backgrounds. It is the mother of all mating signals. Sadly, its use has fallen from view in favor of more verbal or showy displays of interest. This is a very sad state of affairs because people seem to forget that we, as humans, are still animals.

We still have animal like signals and responses similar to other species of the animal kingdom. We, as humans, can give a signal to a potential mate non-verbally which in turn is received as an opportunity to have sex. This is the power of the eyes.

People look, but they do not really see what is going on before them. We look at things all the time, but rarely do we focus or pay really close attention to what we're looking at. More often than not, we never pay attention to the kind of look we give when looking at someone or something. And it is exactly this kind of carelessness that allows the Copulatory Gaze to go unnoticed.

Many men nowadays are more focused on what they are looking at and the information they are receiving from the object of attention. They don't care and are unaware of how they look at women. You must not fall into this state of being. It is vital that you become aware of how you look with your eyes if you are to succeed with women.

The Copulatory Gaze is not just a look you give with your eyes. No, it is also the way your eyes look while giving the look that determines whether or not you will come across as a sexually powerful man or a weird, creepy, stalker guy.

There are many men who admire women with their eyes. It is evident in their gaze, but this is not the Copulatory Gaze which women read as an opportunity for sex. The gaze most men deploy when admiring women with their eyes is that gaze women read as desperate, needy and kind of creepy. Be careful not to fall into this category because once you do, it is very, very difficult to be seen as anything otherwise.

The correct look is to gaze upon the woman, not smiling, not frowned or shaky, but with a look of determination, strength, lust, confidence and analysis.

As you look her over, when her eyes meet yours, let her see herself in your eyes, through your eyes. Your gaze shall not be quick, shifty or hurried.

Let your eyes linger a bit as if stuck by glue. While

your eyes are locked on hers, without removing the gaze, it is best to move your head as if tracing the outside of a square. This is the Ancient method of the Seducer. Women know this gaze instinctively and will respond in kind.

After she has been gazed upon, you can then meet her giggle, movements, or shyness, with a slight smile. A slight smile. Not ever a toothy, goofy grin. Just a slight toothless smile. At this point, you can either engage in a conversation, which she'll more than likely do or you can simply look away. The triggers have been fired where they should go.

Your gaze is not wide-eyed, but soft and relaxed. Not necessarily a squint, but something very close to it. Your gaze is also not a death stare. You are not competing with her to see who can stare at whom the longest.

You must convey an animalistic intensity, yet with the cool, calm and control of a man who knows he could render her to putty in his hands.

While deploying the gaze, you will find the need to blink. You can and must blink, but there is a certain way that even this movement must be done. You must not blink rapidly. Doing so shows nervousness. Your blinking must be slow, as if slowed down by slow motion.

You must show her that you aren't affected by her as much as she is affected by you. Smooth, cool, calm and controlled. Do not be quick to look away from her. This is of the utmost importance. Shifty movements, looking down, smiling or speaking breaks the communication and shows you as weak. It is not until you see her react to your gaze that you look away or start conversation.

Remember, it is not about what you think or feel

when she is locked on to you. It is not about you at this moment, it is about her. This must be evident in your gaze. If she feels that you're more consumed in thoughts about yourself, and could be careless about her, then you are lost.

As inherently selfish creatures, women will know immediately if you are all about them or all about yourself. It is the foolish man who thinks that being the most interesting man he knows will win the favor of women. Nothing could be further from the truth.

The truth is women only care that you are interested in them and their pleasure. But men only see the first part of the equation and go from there.

They act interested, which is good, but then ruin everything by being interested in a bunch of nonsense that doesn't matter. What her favorite color is, where she's from, what kind of music she listens to, is nonsense that does not bring you closer to being her lover. This route will only put you in the friend category.

The real meaning of being interested is seeing women first as women and being interested in their sexual pleasure. This is bedrock. Women don't care what you know. They just need to know that you care. Again, women are inherently selfish creatures. This is in no way a bad thing. It actually gives you a clearly defined way in which you shall deal with women. Once a woman is sexually satisfied, everything else falls into place.

There is a structure to all of this madness. And the actual structure, when it comes to relationships between men and women, is as follows: seduction, sex, then dating. Not dating, seduction, then sex or in any other order.

SOLOMON'S WAY

You cannot re-write thousands of years of documented truth. There shall not be any preliminary screening process which she can employ. A lot of the hoops men have to jump through have been created and put in place by women for men who do not know any better. Men foolishly jump through these hoops thinking they will win, but what fools they are indeed!

When you follow the correct structure, the most Ancient of all structures defined above, you will establish yourself as a powerful, knowledgeable and sexually attractive man. You will hold all the power in your dealings with women. It is not until after you've seduced and pleasured a woman do you decide whether or not you want to make her your girlfriend, wife, friend or all of the above.

Understand that it is not necessary to make a woman anything other than a satisfied lover. Women, not wanting to be alone and instinctively striving to build relationships, will try to convince you that a relationship based on something more than sex is in order. Do not fall for it. Remember, her selfish nature makes her not want to share with you any other woman. This is understandable and how she should feel, but ultimately, it is your decision. You have that power and that's the way it should be.

Once a woman has had a taste of your nectar, she will go to great lengths to taste it again. You shall never worry if she leaves and never returns. Why? Because she represents only one of the many millions that can be yours. She knows this. So, she'd rather stick around and be happy with whatever you decide than be alone and sad without you.

There is nothing wrong with being a sexually active man or having a fleet of women at your disposal. Just look to history if you have doubts. Genghis Khan had well over 3,000 concubines. And that's just one example.

It is safe to say that Genghis knew well of the Ancient method. He also knew of women and their basic nature. Remember, nothing has changed in women from then to now. They are still the same. What has changed is man's thoughts about them and how they now deal with them.

Contrary to what the experts say about body language and posture, you do not need to have an up-right, chest stuck out, uncomfortable posture to attract the opposite sex. You'll only look silly trying to pull this off. Your head shall remain unbowed, face forward, chin not raised so you're looking down your nose, but where your head is level. Your body shall be ever relaxed with your hands to your side or slightly clasped behind your back. This will show you are non-threatening as you are exposing all of your vital organs to her by showing her the whole front side of your body.

You can place more weight on one leg or the other but do not shift from side to side like an idiot. Too much movement on your part will signal to her that she has an effect on your and that you are, therefore, not in control of yourself or the situation.

Like most predatory animals, women can smell fear. They can recognize fear in your eyes, face, voice and body language. A man who is overly animated is not the man women want to ravish them. It is the man whose movements are measured, whose gaze is unwavering, whose posture is relaxed... the man who is confident that he can give a woman what she needs and who sees her as all that matters in this moment. That is the man women want to ravish them.

SOLOMON'S WAY

The laws governing attraction between a man and a woman are hardwired into our brains. The switches and triggers are not something you can buy to add to who you are. They are already within you. Of course, having nice things or a good job or knowing people-in-the-know are nice, but they are not at all necessary.

When the human animal deems it necessary, deems it vital to find a mate, it will rely on what is already embedded in its DNA, the Ancient method. It requires no games, no gimmicks, no nonsense.

Not only is this method Ancient, reliable, and foolproof, it is also the most successful of all methods because it is not contrived. There is no theory involved. Only hardcore science and millions of years of human response. But knowledge is one thing. Application is another.

CHRISTOPHER J. SOLOMON

Women speak a language
men can't seem to hear.

A man must make a woman
the center of his universe for a time.

Who she is, what she is,
where she's from doesn't matter.

5

THE APPLICATION

The knowledge and wisdom of the Seducer has been described and discussed thus far. Now it is time to put everything together in the application.

Perhaps an illustration is in order so you may get a better view of the application and its subtleties. Let's just say that one day you're in a bookstore and a young beautiful woman walks in capturing your attention. Everything that has been put forth concerning your outlook, mindset and demeanor shall instantly be put into place.

Regardless if this woman is looking your way or not, deploy the Copulatory Gaze upon her. Women, naturally wanting to be safe, will look around to check her surroundings. When a woman is in unfamiliar territory, her survival instincts will kick in and she will scan the horizon to be on the lookout for potential danger. She must ensure that she is safe.

All of this happens in a blink of an eye. Once she

processes that she is safe, her biology resorts back to baseline. She is on the prowl now to see who can satisfy her.

It is in this moment that your Gaze upon her will be noticed. She will notice your Gaze and you will lock eyes. Contact has been made. Now, she, not really wanting to have a staring contest with you, will look down, breaking the eye-contact as she does.

Now, what happens in the next three seconds is critical to your sexual success with this woman. As you keep your eyes on her after she has looked down, one of two things will happen; she will look back up to meet your Gaze again or she won't.

If she looks back up to meet your Gaze, that is your signal to approach her. If she does not look back up within those three seconds, DO NOT APPROACH!!! We'll get back to this last part in a moment, but first the approach.

Once you receive the green light to approach, there is no need to make circles when a straight line will suffice. You may make circles if you want to stall or beat around the bush, but each minute you waste is a minute you could use to add a woman to your growing fleet. Or it could be a minute you waste and your opportunity is lost.

So, upon receiving the green light, you approach her without a minute to waste. Introduce yourself, and you in turn get her name, if she hasn't reciprocated and given it to you already. While looking into her eyes, tell her that she looks like someone you'd like to get to know better. As in, "Amy, I'd like to get to know you better.. And with that, you give her your phone number. At this point, you can decide whether or not you want her number. She is going to call regardless.

SOLOMON'S WAY

If you want her number, which is always the smart choice, simply say, "I would also like to call you tonight."

This will make her give you her number without having to resort to looking like a fool by asking, "Can I have your number?" It sounds pathetic, looks pathetic, is pathetic.

The reason you can be so confident that she'll comply is because she gave you the green light. This green light is so much more than just a signal to approach. It is a signal that says "yes" to pretty much anything and everything.

If we were living before the invention of phones, you wouldn't be exchanging numbers. You two would be on your way to your dwelling or hers on your way to exchanging bodily fluids. But, in modern times, we must respect public places and social decorum.

Remember, the Copulatory Gaze that you deploy is the oldest and most ancient method. It's nothing new. It's just new to you.

Once you have exchanged numbers with this beautiful young woman, lightly grasp her hand and lightly give the back of it a soft kiss. At that same moment, call her by her name and tell her that it has been a pleasure meeting her. And that you'll talk to her later. Then, simply turn and leave or go back to doing whatever it was you were doing beforehand. It is that simple.

Now, let's dissect this interaction. First, there should be no hesitation on your part to approach after you've been given the green light. Why? Because it can trigger self-doubt in a woman. It can make her think that what she saw in your Gaze was not what she really thought.

If you hesitate, it leaves the possibility open for her to leave or someone stepping into the picture complicating things. Every situation has its own set of circumstances.

For instance, if you know that she works there at the store, then you can stand to wait a few minutes before approaching. She's not going anywhere soon and you can pace yourself. For the most part, though you want to approach quickly. Don't miss your opportunity.

Once you've approached, introduced yourself and got her name, it is best to be direct in your intentions. Being direct means being bold which in turn means being confident. And being confident is what matters most.

A man who is unable to be bold and take control is a man women find unattractive.

Talking around what is really going on early on only shows that you're uncomfortable with the situation. Sure, being indirect and engaging in playful banter is perfect for a romantic comedy, but not for a Seducer.

A Seducer provides sexual pleasure. Romance and relationships do not factor into the equation. These two things are secondary to the primary purpose, which is to provide sexual pleasure.

There is no need to feel guilty or self-conscious about your purpose. It is your right as a man to define things on your terms concerning the women with whom you engage in sexual relations.

Women expect men to lead. Women expect men to initiate everything. Women expect men to do what men are supposed to do and that is to pursue, pamper and pleasure them.

After you have met her and obtained her number, there will be no question as to your intentions. Many

SOLOMON'S WAY

men make the mistake of trying to come in underneath the radar, being indirect as if a woman is not intelligent enough to realize that he wants to sleep with her.

This is bad for a bunch of reasons, but there are two main reasons 1) being indirect confuses her. She doesn't know if you want to be her lover or if you want to be her gay best friend. And 2) not showing your intentions makes you look indecisive. Women aren't stupid or dumb. They know that on some level you want to have sex with them, whether you know it or not. Just know that they know.

It would be more of a compliment to women if you show your interest from the start. From that point on, they know how to see you. They know how to treat you. They won't be able to put you in the friend category.

Once you are put in the friend category, it is very, very difficult to move on to being a lover. Many men think that by being friendly, becoming a friend and showing no sexual interest in them whatsoever that they can eventually bridge the gap. This is a fatal flaw in our thinking.

It is the friend she sees as non-threatening, the one she can let her hair down around and talk to all day about what's bothering her. This is not the same guy she shares her bed with.

It is far better to announce your intentions from the beginning. That way you won't invest in something from which you'll get no return. Not only is this defeating, but you'll look and feel foolish.

δ δ δ

The beauty of this method of Seduction is that there is no such thing as rejection when you employ the method properly. Remember, if she does not look back up to meet your Gaze within three seconds, DO NOT APPROACH!!!

For whatever reason, she is not looking for a relationship, sexual or otherwise. You save yourself from being rejected and you go on hunting for other females. No one knows of the communication that just took place between you and her so no one's ego is hurt.

We don't need to twist our minds in knots trying to think about what went wrong or whatnot. You'll only think yourself to death because, unless you ask her and she tells you, you'll never know what she thought. So, it doesn't matter. That is what's so awesome about this method. You don't have to worry about anything.

δ δ δ

Most guys who have a lot of confidence can approach a woman out of the blue and make it work. This is not necessarily bad except that usually, these men are not aware of the signals a woman puts out.

She may not be interested in him, but he overlooks that because he is just fulfilling his need to talk to a pretty woman. He doesn't recognize that he is trying to convince her with his talk that he has an interest in her.

Of course, showing her that you are a silver-tongued devil has its perks, but only after some time has passed. Set the right context first and then you can say whatever you want.

SOLOMON'S WAY

A man who talks a lot is not seen by women as sexy. They are seen as gossipy, needy, weak. Speak only when it serves to either reach your goal or to please her. Always make sure she does most of the talking. This will keep you strong and sexy in her eyes.

δ δ δ

Women need a rock, not a sponge. A man who understands this is ahead of the game. Some men think it is necessary to share stories. For instance, she mentions she likes old cartoons. The common, unwise man will jump immediately at the opportunity to say he likes them, too. Then, suddenly, he's rambling on about himself like she actually cares.

What this man should really do is dig further into who she is, what she thinks, and what she feels. Sure, the "me too" things bonds you, but not in a seductive way. It bonds you in the "best friend" kind of way.

This sort of thing is okay later on after you've decided to make her your girlfriend or just a friend, but it does not fly when you're trying to have a relationship with her based on nothing but sex.

You should understand that by following the Ancient method, you will not encounter the same roadblocks or pit-stops that a common man would when pursuing a normal, romantic relationship. All the unnecessary garbage is removed from your path.

You weave your way through the thicket of spider webs with ease to achieve your goal of providing women with sexual pleasure. You will find that getting sex is easier than you thought. And that pursuing a relationship first, is where it gets complicated.

δ δ δ

Relationships are of a woman's world and pursuing sex is of a man's world. It has been said throughout time and it still lingers today: men will give love for sex and women will give sex for love. Although it is true, Seducers never have to stoop so low. We don't have to be deceptive at all with anything.

Those who are not aware of the Ancient method will often resort to the maxim above, but not Seducers. A Seducer can naturally attract the opposite sex, not because of methods or tricks of the trade, but because Seducers know that it all comes from within.

You must project a
certain kind of confidence,
a sexual confidence.

Biology hasn't changed
in men or women.

6

THE EXCUSES

Sometimes in the game of Seduction the Seducer doesn't have to pursue the woman. Sometimes the Seducer is pursued by the woman. These conquests are some of the most enjoyable and most fulfilling because most of your work is done for you.

Of course, you still must perform your role as a Seducer, but in instances like this, you don't have to hunt. Your women fall right into your hands. In order for situations like this to happen, you must be able to recognize the signs. You must be able to recognize the "EXCUSES."

An excuse is any reason a woman uses to interact with you or engage you in conversation.

A very common theme used in conjunction with an excuse or as a stand-alone tactic women employ is "proximity." Proximity is a woman standing or being in the general area of where you are.

Because of a woman's inherent need to be safe, she

is always aware of her surroundings. This not only means that she is aware of the area where she stands, this also means she's aware of the men and women present in this area.

Seven to ten feet is a safe distance for a woman, or anyone for that matter, to stand from a perfect stranger without being intrusive or bothersome.

When a woman is interested in someone, she will instinctively stand closer to them, somewhere around five feet or less. Proximity is anywhere within this five foot radius.

A woman will stand in proximity to you in hopes that you will engage her somehow, either through acknowledgment of her presence and/or initiating conversation with her. Many times if you don't understand what's going on, she will take it upon herself to engage you and initiate conversation. Chances like this should not be missed.

There are plenty of excuses a woman will use in conjunction with proximity. For example, she may ask for the time, pretend to fiddle with something, or even drop something just to get your attention.

She may leave something of hers at your house, in your car, or even on you. She may ask about a mutual friend, a mutual enemy, or an otherwise off-the-wall question.

These are all excuses. Women employ these with the skill and frequency of a skilled Army General, at will, and with devastating effect.

$$\delta \; \delta \; \delta$$

Just as a woman's words can deceive, so too can a woman's actions. What may seem like a casual situation may actually be a sign of interest on her part.

So, if recognition is of primary importance and the first part of the equation, then capitalizing on the situation is secondary and the last part of the equation.

Once you recognize the excuse or excuses, because sometimes they come in groups, you must be able to capitalize. Seeing that most of your work is done for you, this part shouldn't be difficult.

First, acknowledge her, either through eye contact and a slight toothless smile, or a verbal answer if she has broken the silence herself. What you must never do is be critical of her presence, questioning, or clumsiness. Women are women, not men. So, what may seem cool to guys is not cool with them. Accept her.

Now that you're both aware of each other's presence, one of two things will happen: she will either extend the conversation until you show your interest in her or she will try to end the conversation or interaction hoping that you will show your interest in her.

In the event that she stays to extend the interaction, she is already aware of what she is going to say and will provide the topics for conversation. What she's basically doing is auditioning for you. She's going to highlight her best traits in a short amount of time.

While she is on stage, you must keep your responses within the realm of a traditional Seducer. This means you do the following: you paraphrase what she just said, you nod your head, you say "uh-huh," "right" and "I understand." Not all at once, of course, but you choose one from this list of responses every time she says something.

SOLOMON'S WAY

This is the true art of listening. You do not try to dominate the conversation, telling her stories of how awesome you are or think you are. This does not impress women. It makes you look like an idiot.

All you have to do is listen, and believe it or not, it gets interpreted as talking about her. This is good because women, being inherently selfish, love to hear all about themselves.

When there is a break from her talking and/or when you feel she's about to end the interaction, tell her that she seems like someone you'd like to get to know better.

From there you can pause to let her respond or you can immediately follow-up with telling her you want to call her tonight. Her responses in both cases shall be the same: she'll give you the information you need to contact her. Now, your job is done until you meet again.

Now, let's say she tries to end the conversation or interaction. Sometimes women will do this, not because they are not interested, but because sometimes they feel a little embarrassed, a little self-conscious about being in your presence. This happens when a woman is really drawn to a man sexually.

She'll seem a little nervous. She may shake, quiver, check her nails and generally want to get away. This is not a bad thing. It just shows the effect you have on her. It is always good to have an effect on women because it's more primal and less superficial.

δ δ δ

Women like to feel like they are the prize. They want to be chased and not feel like they are giving themselves up to you so freely. Of course, we know this is what they are doing, but as long as they feel they are not, that's all that matters.

So, give them little chase. When you see that she is about to leave, stop her. Tell her that she looks like someone you'd like to get to know better and that you'd like to call her tonight.

This response seems repetitive, but there is no need to complicate matters when a simple tried and true response will do. She will reply with her information.

Then, take her hand, give it a kiss and let her leave. She'll be too over-whelmed to stay so she'll leave quickly. Your part is done for now. You've capitalized and that is what is most important.

Sometimes it will be convenient to recognize when you must offer her a reason to offer an excuse, opportunities like these pop-up more often than you realize. Sometimes a woman may want to see you in order to have her biological desire satisfied, but does not know of another excuse to use to see you. That is when you offer or help her out with an excuse.

For instance, let's say you're at home and she calls you. Not having anything to really talk about, she tries to make a small-talk. You know what she really wants to hear and what her intentions are. Help her out by saying something like, "I want you to come over. I have some interior design issues I need you to help me out with."

Of course, anything will work so long as you supply a reason for their excuse as to why she had sex with you. This is only to assuage her critical mind.

When she speaks of this encounter later to her

SOLOMON'S WAY

girlfriends, it sounds much better when she says, "I was helping him with such and such," rather than "I went over there to get sexed down."

These kinds of excuses can come from the intended women you want to bed and/or her friends, acquaintances, co-workers, whoever really has no business seeing you, but desperately wants to see you. Help them out. Offer them an excuse.

Focus, not on yourself
but on women.

Nothing is above you or her.

THE ANSWERS

So far we have discussed the method and the application. Now it is time to discuss the answers. The culmination of all your efforts—the Seduction.

This is where you must prove your desire for her. This is where you must show her that you can and will take care of her sexual pleasure, that you are the real deal and not just a man trying to fulfill your own sexual desires.

It must be understood that it is the man's job to lead. What this means is you show no uncertainty in anything you do. You must move with assurance. If you display uncertainty, it will make her protective side creep and she'll question herself as to why she's there with you. She'll begin to question whether you can provide the pleasure you projected.

When you move with certainty and confidence, she will relax and feel comfortable with you. She'll know instinctively that she'll be protected and provided for.

Therefore, no shifty, shaky or fidgety movements. You must show no signs of nervousness or self-consciousness. This is of the utmost importance.

When a woman has agreed to be alone with you, she has agreed to your production. This means that she is very well aware of what can happen just by being there with you alone.

Therefore, there shall be no fear in moving with the energy of a man with sexual desire. Of course, this does not mean stripping naked or exposing yourself. Such actions are not of the Seducer, but of the crazy sex fiend women are afraid of.

What this means is you do not stop projecting the desire you have for her. The look in your eyes shall be the same as when you first eyed her. The difference between then and now is now you're going to show her that you mean business.

δ δ δ

Upon arriving at your dwelling, you shall make physical contact with her by taking her hand and kissing her cheek. This will make her feel relaxed as you have not waited to touch her nor did you make a big deal out of touching her.

You should make her feel even more relaxed by taking her coat if she has one, and invite her to sit down on the couch with you. You can offer her a drink if time permits, but this is not necessary. Once she is seated, quickly take a seat right beside her.

The point is to show no hesitation and no awkwardness in being near her. Remember, the point

SOLOMON'S WAY

of her being there is to be with you, not to talk about the weather, or politics. So move with the boldness of a man who truly understands women.

Quickly seize her by the hand and ask her how she is. While she answers, begin to slowly kiss the back of her hand. If her answer is short, ask her another question that requires a longer answer. Something like, "How was your day?" will suffice. It's not really about what she says. You're just breaking the silence.

As she continues to answer, continue to kiss her hand: the front, the back, between her fingers, individual fingers. For women, the hand is a very intimate body part. What you do with it and how you treat it is noticed by her. It's like giving her a preview of what you intend to do with her body.

Once you have spent a few moments on her hand, begin to move to her wrist. The wrist is an even more vulnerable spot. You can tell how comfortable a woman is by how she exposes her wrist.

Instinctively, humans hide the most vulnerable points in their body when there is a threat and expose those same points to that which they are comfortable with.

Continue kissing her wrist while slowly making your way up her forearm. Her hand should still be within your grasp being pulled above your shoulder, behind your head. Once you reach her inner elbow, kiss and nuzzle this area as this is another very sensitive spot.

You will begin to see a change in her breathing; it is becoming slower and deeper. Her eyes will dilate and at this point, she may stop talking, her mind forgetting what was being said.

It is from here that you move in slowly, looking her in the eye, then her lips as you kiss her. It is best to cradle her head as you kiss her, but it is not absolutely necessary as long as you keep physical contact with her body somehow. Cradling her head makes her feel safe and cared for.

The kiss shall not be a quick kiss, but a slow sensual kiss. Do not probe her mouth with an over-eager inexperienced teenage tongue, but with a loving, caressing, massaging tongue. Guide her tongue to unite with yours. Speak to her with your tongue. You can tell her all she needs to know about you with just your kiss alone.

Make her feel like she can kiss you all day long. Tease her with your tongue. Toy with her. Make her expect it then pull it away. Move your tongue slowly, confidently. Don't dart it around and don't try to shove it down her throat. Show mastery with your tongue and she will khow you are a master.

Kiss her like all that matters in the entire world is right there, right now. You can trigger her arousal immediately with just your kiss alone if done correctly.

Close your eyes as you kiss her. Women naturally do this, but sometimes they like to keep their eyes open. Closing your eyes will make her do the same. Having her eyes closed will allow her to focus on the feeling within her body and not visual information her eyes would take in.

The kiss alone will prepare for sex, but you must not rush things. Women love the slow burn. Ten to twenty seconds is good, initially. A one to two second pause should elapse before you lock lips again. This time, however, this kiss should last for two minutes or more.

As you continue kissing her, slowly move your hands to her clothes to remove them. Slowly move her and yourself to a laying position. Continue with your sweet kisses as you begin to take her clothes off. Each time a large portion of flesh is revealed, take your time to appreciate it with loving kisses before moving back to her lips.

Tender kisses upon her neck, shoulder, collarbone and chest will always bode well. These are always spots you can return to in order to keep her aroused.

Once her shirt and bra are off, you then remove your shirt. Continue to focus on her mouth as you take the rest of her clothes off. Remember there is no need to hurry. Do not show eagerness in your movements.

Once she is out of everything, take your time to appreciate her beauty in all its glory. Give her body a slow once over taking in all her lovely curves before returning to her gaze with a smile. Kiss her deeply, before slowly trailing down her neck to her breasts, her tummy, the top of her thighs, the inside of her thighs, her knees, her calf muscles, her ankles. Praise her entire body leaving her most feminine area for last.

Remember, it is about her pleasure, not yours. When you take your time, it shows you are not a selfish lover, but a generous one. If you are forever giving pleasure, you will always receive pleasure.

Some women like to receive oral pleasure whereas some women do not. A woman's insecurities about herself or her body are not something you can try to understand so you should not try.

If you see an effort on her part to stop you from pleasing her orally, simply continue back up her body to her lips. There is no need to force the issue. Your efforts will not go unnoticed. They will be appreciated. She knows what she likes. If you feel she wants it, then proceed as follows.

Take a positon between her legs with her inches away

from your face. Begin to kiss the first set of lips you see. Slowly spread these lips to reveal the smaller inner lips. Now, if she has been properly aroused, the outer lips will move to reveal these inner lips automatically which in turn expose her opening.

Begin to kiss and lick around the outside taking care to focus around the top which is where the famed clitoris is located.

The clitoris may be slightly exposed resembling a little pink button. This button is surrounded by a fleshy hood. It is here that the majority of nerve endings for pleasure are located. Slowly cup your mouth over this area, your tongue pressed flat over the button.

Slowly move your tongue back and forth from side to side. Pay attention to your woman and the responses she gives. This will determine what you do with your tongue.

If you see she responds better to your movements when you go back and forth, then you shall stay on this path. No need to change course if this path will take her to Orgasmland.

You can further enhance your woman's response by slowly sliding two fingers, preferably the index and middle fingers of your left hand, inside of her. Slowly sliding them in with fingers straight and pulling them out slightly curled toward the ceiling is the motion you want.

Your mouth on her clitoris, your fingers inside of her, your right hand pressed on her tummy or breasts is the optimal position.

Once you build and lock on to the right rhythm that has her responding with loud moaning, heavy breathing, lip licking, closed eyes, and arched back, continue in the same fashion until you bring her to orgasm. You

SOLOMON'S WAY

will know you've reached this point when she stiffens and convulses underneath you turning to goo. She'll be shaky and out of breath, at a loss for energy.

At this point, you may want to continue, but beware; the clitoris is extremely sensitive after orgasm and it may take a moment or two before she can take another dose of sweet torture.

Allowing her to recover, begin to kiss her body lovingly as you make your way back to her face. Of course, you should use caution when going near her face with your mouth. Some women do not want to taste themselves on your lips nor do they even want to think about it.

So, keep your kisses on her body. She'll let you know by lifting your head up that she wants to kiss you.

Now, what comes next is up to you. You could let this session be all about her and forgo actual sex. If this is so, go the kitchen and grab a glass of ice water. ALWAYS HAVE ICE WATER ON HAND!!! Bring this glass of ice water to her. This is for her to drink. This gesture alone shows that you're very attentive to her needs, before and after play.

If she is not all spent from the beautiful orgasm that you have just given her and wants you inside of her then you must oblige.

First and foremost, you must show her that you care about her safety and yours by pulling out a condom. Regardless if she wants to use one or not, one who pleases women does not need interference with his work.

After you have completely undressed, put the condom on and move onto her body. Continue with your kisses up her body while you penetrate her slowly. Slowly move in and out of her, reading her as you do.

Move from side to side, varying your thrusts: short, short, deep, deep, deep, short, etc. Move in a circular motion. Massage her on the inside. She may even tell you what she wants you to do. Faster, slower, deeper are not criticisms, but verbal expression of what she likes.

A true Seducer pays attention and adjusts his technique accordingly. Once she exhibits the traits as before, lock on to what you're doing and don't stray from it. She does not need distraction. She needs focus to orgasm.

Once she orgasms, hold on to her and try to orgasm at the same time if you can. If not, fear not. Let her turn to mush in your arms. Kiss her tenderly and hold her for a few moments as she gets her energy back. When the moment is right, leave to retrieve the ice water mentioned before. Bring her the ice water.

Sit with her for as long as she needs. Normally, after the "after glow," has worn off, she'll want to retreat to the restroom. Let her go.

It is in this moment you'll get yourself together and straighten back up. It would be wise to pop a breath mint or freshen your breath somehow. When she returns, it is yet another scene from her play.

Upon her return, greet her with a long, sensual kiss. Your job is done. From here, she can stay, leave or whatever.

In the initial sexual encounter with her, you want to keep things a little Rated R as opposed to Rated X. The reason you begin with Rated R is because you do not want to frighten her away with your explicit sexual nature.

She's just now coming to know you sexuality. Of course, you will find some who are sexually aggressive and will want to do some X-rated things. In those cases, you will follow her lead. But as a general rule, proceed with caution. Start off with a Rated R and move on to Rated X as each encounter comes along.

The change of positions, changes of locations, and the change of speed,. will come about as she feels more comfortable with you. You don't want to have sex like a porn star with a woman you just met unless she indicates otherwise. The point is to pleasure her, to make your penis become her best friend. You do not try to punish her with your penis. That kind of situation may come about later. Make her look forward to being pleasured. Give it in doses and she'll be coming back for more.

Sometimes the situation may call for something quick. In instances like these, you may forgo her oral pleasure and go straight for penetrative sex. Usually, if all she has is a few moments to spare, she's not looking to get licked up but sexed down.

Notice how through all of this, there was no mention of your own personal pleasure. The reason is because it is not about you. It is about her. Through pleasuring her, you will be pleased, especially when you recognize the frequency at which you get to pleasure her.

Women are selfish creatures mostly because their needs are rarely met. When their needs are met, they will give of themselves and of everything else freely just to show how much they appreciate you. You'll be the keeper of her pleasure. It will be your responsibility.

Sometimes you may be called to her dwelling. In those cases, focus intently on the woman. Make your surroundings disappear. She is already comfortable enough that she doesn't need any settling in. You can go in boldly.

She'll be more comfortable in a place of her choosing or her personal dwelling because she knows that much more about it than you do. Some guys can easily become distracted by a woman's bedroom or house and begin to feel like all of her belongings are judging them, but they aren't. This feeling is easily overcome by putting in a little more effort in pleasing her.

A little more effort means completely overwhelming her with sexual desire. Take her to heights she's not used to, heights she's never been to, beyond Venus and Mars on toward Saturn.

Make it an experience she'll never forget and one she'll love re-telling to her friends. This is the job description of a Seducer. You provide sexual pleasure. Nothing less and anything more is of your choosing.

A Seducer provides
sexual pleasure.

A true Seducer loves
and cherishes women like no other.

8

THE HEADACHES

A Seducer will experience plenty of headaches. Headaches may come in the form of women wanting to reform you, women wanting to make you their boyfriend or their husband, women wanting to possess you and women wanting to have you all to themselves.

The root cause of your headaches will be women. This is not necessarily a bad thing, but it can be if you allow it.

Women, being all that they are, will give of themselves freely and willingly. This is all good, but one must remember that beneath the pretty exterior, women are inherently selfish. What this means in this sense, is that women will still want a little something in return. This little something they want is a relationship.

By relationship, we mean something more than just a sexual relationship. Why? Because in her mind, it will not only justify her ways with you, but it will also fulfill her need to be loved.

SOLOMON'S WAY

Once she has you in a relationship, she grows in power. Her natural strength lies in the world of relationships. Once you're in her world, she'll be able to have full control of you. And as an added bonus, she'll be the one who gets to tell you what to do and when to do it.

When this happens, she'll begin to withhold sex for ransom and this is not what you want. Your days of being Seducer will be far behind once you let this happen.

A woman's power lies in her ability to create and maintain relationships. And within these relationships, she is able to excel, to create tension, create intrigue, to create hope and hopelessness, to create whatever it is her heart desires because she is now the puppet master. The complexities of these relationships where she is master are beyond the scope of your interest. Do not lose your focus.

This is just something to be aware of. You'll also have headaches that are more enjoyable. You'll have women who will want to possess you. Why? Because what you give out, sexual pleasure, will become like a drug to them. They will want it more and more as time passes.

Humans, being creatures of routine, will make a habit out of anything done repetitively for sixty-three days. This means that after two months, she'll be in the habit of receiving pleasure at certain times of the day. So, be careful with how much pleasure you give. Casanova was mindful, you should be also.

The problem with a woman who tries to possess you is she'll come around unexpectedly at inopportune times, all the time. She'll show up when you may have another woman at your lair. This can cause some drama for you, but you'll be all right.

You owe no one an explanation for anything. This is where most men begin back-pedaling when the women pull their emotional guns on him. You must not fall into this trap. You are guilty of nothing except spreading pleasure like a honeybee spreads pollen.

Usually, the women will turn their sights on each other, reckoning within themselves that you are not at fault for anything. You are just doing what you do. Now, depending on what kind of woman you have, you could see a good old catfight. Or not.

Sometimes it's good that one woman knows about the other. Usually, that's when one will try to prove herself more worthy than the other. She'll begin her show, trying to out-perform the other. Her hopes are that she'll succeed and as a result you'll stop seeing the other woman.

Let her think what she wants, but never give her a verbal confirmation that you'll stop. If you do and you keep seeing the other woman, then you'll just be a liar. And the Seducer does not need to lie.

Women, believe it or not, do not need to be lied to when it comes to matters regarding sex. Only the lowly and lonely will sink that low in order to get sex.

A Seducer does not, ever, sink that low. How can one call himself a Seducer if he uses deception? The women can fight, try to put on their best sexual performance for you, even stalk you, but in the end, you are still the same as you were when you met them: a Seducer.

They will not hate you, do not fear. You'll be respected, adored, and even worshipped. Let the women drive themselves crazy over you while you remain stoic. This can go on forever if you want it to, with as many women as you want.

Be not afraid of numbers. The more numbers you

have, the more you'll be revered by men and women alike. Men will want to be you, while women will want to be with you. This is nothing to be ashamed of. This is something to be proud of.

It has been a longstanding and unspoken belief that a man who can possess women at will is a man who can possess the world at will. This is as it should be. A Seducer shall possess the world, not through force, but through his mastery of women. It is the Seducer's birthright.

A true Seducer possesses
the wisdom and knowledge
of Seducer's past.

We miss 99% of what is said to us.
H.I.S. Goddess
needs to be unleashed.

THE NINE FUNDAMENTAL CHARACTERICS OF A TRUE SEDUCER

1. A true Seducer loves and cherishes women like no other.
2. A true Seducer's sole purpose is to provide sexual pleasure to women and ultimately unleash their Inner Sex Goddess.
3. A true Seducer does not beg, lie, or deceive women in order to have sex with them.
4. A true Seducer's focus is on women, not on himself.
5. A true Seducer's demeanor is always cool, calm and collected. He does not let the emotions of others affect him.
6. A true Seducer's success is not based on appearance, material wealth, social status or belongings. His success is based on his unique understanding of women.

7. A true Seducer possesses the wisdom and knowledge of Seducers past.
8. A true Seducer has the potential to possess the world through his mastery of women.
9. A true Seducer has choice in the type and number of women he decides to pleasure. He is a god amongst women.

Women are experts
on reading emotions.

Women are smarter than
what you give them credit for.

10

THE SEXUAL POWER OF NAMES

Many people over-look the sexual significance of someone's first name. We call names carelessly not really understanding what they reveal about the owner.

Modern day names have lost the magical, sexual element that the names of the past had. The reason is people nowadays have to think of names to name their children.

They want to be different and stand apart from the norm. So they choose or create a name that will excite or cause people to talk.

Most names, up until about the mid1990s, had roots that dated back to biblical times. The further back you go, the more biblical the names were. These names had meaning to them and as such, when a child was named something like James, this child would exhibit traits that a "James" of the past possessed. That was the magical element of names.

SOLOMON'S WAY

Beyond the topical meaning of someone's name, there also lies an undercurrent to names that has to deal with the sexual nature of the holder and the effect their name has on the opposite sex.

It has only been discovered recently that a man's first name is a good indicator of how many sexual partners he has had or will have. Studies have proven that male names ending in "s" have had more partners than anyone else. The name to top that list is Chris. The letter "s" triggers something primal in the female species. Seeing that a woman's mind will go sexual at any given instant, the letter "s" gets associated with their favorite activity.

Other male names that are effective in effortlessly subduing women are:

    James
    Charles
    Dennis
    Elias
    Alex*

*Although this name does not end in S, the last two letters imply

Names that are less effective at attracting the opposite sex are:

    Edward
    Dylan
    Frank
    Jason
    Grant
    Peter

On the flipside, there are women's names that will give you deep insight into their sexuality. Of course, you already possess the keys to capture any woman's sexuality but you can easily narrow your work down and know what kind of woman you're dealing with simply by knowing her first name.

This may seem new to you and it is. This is knowledge that is meant for only Gods of Seduction. A woman's name is designed to be feminine and the perfect counterpart to our masculine names. Most of the time, a woman's name will take on endings that imply a sense of helplessness. Helplessness is an attractive trait to the male human as it is in his nature to protect.

Names imply helplessness in two ways: ending with the "EE" sound and ending with the "UH" sound. For instance, names with the "EE" sound such as Brandi, Candy, Staci, Cherie, and Aimee fall into the first category, category A.

Melissa, Corina, Lisa, Jessica, etc. fall into the second category, category B.

And finally there are those names that are feminine, but come without the helplessness. These are the names of women that can be soft yet confident and firm in their stance: Michelle, Rachel, Crystal, April, etc. these names that sound like they end in a consonant fall into the last category, category C.

First and foremost, the general sexual temperament for A, B and C is the same as described before as they are all women and are designed the same. But there are subtle differences.

Women with category A names like to have sex as much as the next woman, but are the quickest to fall in love as a result. The frequency in which these women have sex can match your need or even exceed your need so one must take caution with how much and how often you pleasure these types.

Generally, category A's will have sex even when

SOLOMON'S WAY

romantically involved with another man and it won't disturb their conscience one bit.

Women in this category may easily become a headache for you in that they'll want to possess you. Again, this is not always a bad thing. A's are very loving and desire love in return. They feel that when they give of themselves, love is on the way. A's may also assume easily that you two are in a relationship because of your sexual relationship.

Although they won't necessarily come right out and say it, or ask it, they'll allude to it through doing things together, like shopping, living together, picking things out together or generally, doing all the things together that a boyfriend and girlfriend would do together. This can be fine if this is what you want.

Not allowing any of these things to take place in the first place is okay if this isn't what you're looking for. Limit your time together. Limit sleep-overs; limit your actual time together.

By doing this, the nature of your of your relationship will be clearly defined as nothing more than sexual. If you do begin to see more of a woman, it is not wise to lead her on into thinking that you'll change your ways and be with her romantically. This is very dirty and only hurts women.

She'll respect you more if you're open and honest with her from the beginning. She'll know exactly what to expect from you.

Moving on to category B's, the Amandas, Lisas, Jessicas, Juliannas, love to have sex and are not ashamed of it. These are the ones that you'll find more willing than the others to have one night stands.

These are the one you shall seek out when you want to have sex for your pleasure. The care-free spirit and nature of B's is most intoxicating indeed, especially when you experience just how sexually uninhibited these types are.

You'll find that women of category B are far more aware of their Inner Sex Goddess than women from other categories. These women are the ones that men will fall in love with easily after one sexual encounter. So be not surprised if these women have men at their feet willing to do whatever for them at a moment's notice.

This shall not distract you though. These men hope to be rewarded with sex, but their efforts will fall short due to their displays of weakness. It is these guys to whom she'll complain. And most of these complaints will be about you.

Category C women are usually the most difficult to deal with. They are crossbreed between A and B with the added benefit of confidence, high confidence. These women usually know exactly what they want sexually and aren't afraid to voice it.

Category C's are quick to tell you what you're doing right, what you are doing wrong and what you need to do more of. This shall not be taken as a criticism of your technique, but as an uninhibited verbal expression of what works for them

Every woman has a certain movement or series of movements that works to bring her to orgasm, guaranteed, as she is just letting you in the secret of her pleasure.

It is this kind of woman with whom sex is a pleasure because by knowing themselves so well, they are more open to sexual expression. They don't mind being loud or thrashing all over the place in pure delight. But be forewarned: these women are known for using sex for power so do not be alarmed if after your sexual encounter she quickly kicks you out of her dwelling or quickly leaves your dwelling.

Once provided for sexually, they are on to whatever it is they have to do, that part of her being satisfied and shut down. If you let your ego become involved when dealing with this kind of women, you will fall into her web.

Remember, how she is or who she is has nothing to do with you. You've served your purpose so be done with it. Do not let your ego become involved.

Once you become acquainted with the sexual behavior of women from categories A, B and C, you may discover that you prefer a certain type. This is normal. Seducers usually have a certain preference after a while, even though he may still have other types knocking at his door at 2 o'clock in the morning. It is the Seducer's right to have choice over who he deems worthy of his pleasure.

There is a special case of women whose names do not fall into any of the categories mentioned. Those whose names are rare, but end with "O" or "U" or these sounds. Women with these names are very strong mentally and like to have that acknowledged somehow before becoming sexual.

They love to have sex, but need to be freed mentally before the circuits in their body can be fired up. The Clio's and Lanu's can be as uninhibited as category C's but you must help their minds shut down first.

Talking to her, telling her how beautiful and smart she is works well for these types. Words are powerful for any woman, but more so with them.

Although they are confident, because they think so much, it makes them feel less secure. But your words can build her up to where she needs to be.

Women from this category are fun and fun to be with but as with category C's, do not let your ego become involved in the situation. These women may possess a certain knowledge that you do not understand.

Sometimes, after a lot of experience, you'll be able to tell what a woman's first name is or what category it falls into just based on a little observation.

By taking note of a woman's behavior, i.e. the fluidity of her movements, movements that are exaggerated, the amount of eye contact she makes, where she looks with her eyes, the way she uses her words, etc., you'll be able to gauge her general amount of confidence.

Once you do this, you'll be able to deduce which category she fits into. This is not necessary, of course, but you can amuse yourself with your accuracy.

There are many women out there who feel they don't fit their first name and, as such, prefer to go by another name, a nickname of sorts.

The reason is because, just as a brunette will go blonde because "blonds have more fun," so too, would a Marlene becomes a "Marli" or a Michelle becomes "Elle" or a Jennifer becomes a "Jenna" or "Jenni."

Making such changes, especially when a woman begins to introduce herself as such, will reap her great rewards although her general temperament will stay the same, she'll begin to take on a new personality due, not only to how the women treat her, but also because of how the men will begin to receive her.

Based on sound alone, a "Jenna" sounds more fun to play with than a "Jennifer." Jenna's sexual temperament will become that of category B's but only temporarily. Of course, there are exceptions, but none that would spark our immediate interests.

Your demeanor must be cool,
calm and collected.

The gaze is a look of determination,
strength, lust, confidence and analysis.

THE WORLD THROUGH HER EYES THE SECRETS OF EYE CONTACT

Before the invention of language, man had been seducing women the world over without the initial use of pretty words. Although not completely aware of it, man still holds that kind of power even today.

Just as a man can be distracted by a woman's words, he can also become blind to what a woman says with her eyes. Women can speak so clearly with just the look in their eyes that a common man can miss what's being said.

A true Seducer is able to recognize and read what a woman says with her eyes. He has to because his very success with women depends on what she doesn't say with her mouth. It depends on what she says with her eyes.

SOLOMON'S WAY

The eyes are windows to the world for all of us. And as much as woman can see the world through these windows, you can also see into them straight to her Inner Sex Goddess.

This is why it is paramount that you maintain eye contact. Among people in public, you can reach her Goddess through a look alone that only you and she are aware of. It will be your secret world; she knows you want to ravish her and she knows she wants to be ravished. There isn't a care beyond that. That is all that is important.

Sometimes you may not be able to approach the way you want, but may come in contact with a woman by other means. The method still applies, but you may not be able to be as forward as you want with her because of other people; her company or yours being present.

It is in cases like these that you speak to her and listen to her through your eyes. When engaging in eye-contact with her, you must make sure you do not ruin your look by making a face or smiling. This totally negates anything you try to do sexually and pushes you closer into the friend zone.

By making a face you're showing her that you are not comfortable with the eye-contact. She reads this as you not being confident. If you show her that you are not uncomfortable and totally secure with your desires for her, she will begin to feel you are reading her thoughts and desires.

This is exactly what you want to happen. Her mind will begin racing through different sexual scenarios. She'll begin to imagine what can happen in the next few moments. She'll be ready to play out her very own romance/erotica novel.

One must remember that at the core of a woman's biology lies sexual pleasure, Her Inner Sex Goddess. Being able to see the Goddess within her will show her that you understand and can fulfill her needs.

Your eye-contact need not be at maximum where you can't take your eyes off of her. It should be measured like speaking a sentence: hold it a few seconds, look away, look back for less than before, and so on. Of course, this shouldn't be done in rapid succession like a fool, but slow measured, confident. It should be noted that looking at a woman when she speaks, even if she is not looking or speaking to you directly, the attention is interpreted as eye-contact and bodes very well for you. She feels that you can't take your eyes off of her. Always a plus.

Each time you look her way, it should be as if you're saying to her what you will do to her. The first look, you'll take her clothes off with your teeth. The second look, from head to toe, you'll caress every part in between with your tongue. The third, you'll take her against the wall ...

This is a world that only you and she occupy. There is no room for anyone else, and nothing is more important than her at this moment. It is this world people tend to over-look in favor of appealing to someone else's attention. When this happens, that world you could have shared with her disappears.

This shows blatant disregard for her sexual pleasure which is pretty much like a slap in the face to her.

Many men seem to think that women put men in the friend zone. This is only partially true. A man blind to the secrets will usually end up in the friend zone even if his intention was otherwise.

He is oblivious to his actions and the impact they

impart on the opposite sex. It is not his fault, though. Schools don't teach this in classrooms. A Seducer, on the other hand, knows that if a woman is his friend, it is of his own doing, not hers.

A Seducer can and shall have female friends but these friends stem from having already taken them to Orgasmland and/or women you are in the process of taking.

Most, you will find are women you've already taken to Orgasmland. Your friendship will be unique. It will be based on the fact that you've given her a glimpse of home and therefore, you can always take her back there to this wonderful place.

A man must never feel guilty for having an abundance of women. It is a Seducer's right as a man and a man's right as a Seducer.

δ δ δ

The most important features to a woman, on her face are her eyes and her lips. Her eyes are the windows to her entire sexual world. This is the reason so much emphasis is on eye-contact as being an important factor in judging a man's confidence.

Women spend billions each year in cosmetics. The biggest items are those that help her eyes stand out and those that help present a beautiful set of lips. Once the eyes have done their job in attracting a male, the lips come into play as a more subtle reminder of the lips below.

Women everywhere try to do their best to bring out their eyes and their lips when getting dolled-up. And those who don't need any make-up or lipstick are those whose eyes already draw enough attention and whose lips are plump and inviting.

Naturally, without make-up, woman's eyes and lips are enough to draw us in, but women love to play dress-up and as a result, they feel that much more empowered when they add extra emphasis to their eyes and lips.

It should be noted that eye-contact does not just mean looking into her eyes. It also means looking at her lips. By looking at the face from eyes to her lips and back to her eyes, or in the triangle of left eye, lips, right eye, will be interpreted as eye-contact.

This works well for Seducers who still feel slightly uncomfortable holding, controlling and directing a woman's undivided attention. Still, nothing is more important than actual eye contact. The triangle shall be used sparingly and not be used as stand-in for actual contact.

A Seducer does not put anything above the women he is to seduce. Only when she is not present does he deal with his man issues and pressing engagements.

There is a receptive look in your eye that she wants to see. This look tells her she'll be taken to heights never imagined.

So, never forget the importance of eye-contact. Your entire sexual career depends on it. You shall become a master of eye-contract after a while, being able to speak the entire language. Do not rush this.

𝔉ollowing the correct structure,
you will establish yourself
as a powerful, knowledgeable
and sexually attractive man.

12

THE SECRETS OF OBSERVATION

To say that people cannot see would be an understatement. People often fail to take notice of the peculiarities of their environment. We trust our surroundings instinctively, not really aware of what's going on around us. This is a shame because if you're not mindful of your surroundings, chance are you're not mindful the women around you.

The saying "you can't judge a book by its cover" is true in the sense that you don't know the effect the book will have on you unless you read it. The saying usually hides the fact that you can learn a few things about a woman through observation alone.

By studying the way a woman moves, you can tell how confident she is and how she feels about herself sexually. Simply observing the fluidity of a woman's movements can tell you everything you need to know.

SOLOMON'S WAY

It should be noted that sex changes men and women. A man who may, at first, have been a geek or nerd or someone who was generally unpopular with women, may now become a Don Juan and totally possessor of women because of sex. And women, who were clumsy, shy, irritated, may now become relaxed, refined and less tense in their body and their mind. This is what sex can do but only if done correctly, meaning the man and the woman both experience sex the way it was meant to be experienced.

For the man, it shall be a crowning victory of pursuit, of purpose, of pleasure and pride in fulfilling the needs of his woman.

And for the woman, it shall be a journey to this place that all women love: ORGASMLAND.

A woman who is satisfied sexually is satisfied completely. As is often the case, though, the man nor the woman experience sex the way they should. The signs begin to show in every other area of their being, their body being the most affected.

A woman who has been to Orgasmland frequently and/or has had her Inner Sex Goddess unleashed is a woman who moves with the fluidity and grace of an Ethereal being.

There is no hesitancy in her step, no problem too big that she cannot overcome, no reason to worry about anything. She is confident, she is glowing, she longs to return back home to Orgasmland whenever the moment arises.

On the flipside, a woman whose only experiences with sex have been to the man's delight and not her own, her personality may become a little irritable.

The reason for this is because she has been fooled by selfish lovers into thinking she would soon return to Orgasmland. This begins to wear on her.

Her Inner Sex Goddess never has a chance to emerge. She stays in hiding, locked away deep within her vessel. She cradles herself in comfort until the day comes when she can be set free.

Each moment that the Inner Sex Goddess isn't set free, furthers the ill effects on the woman. Minutes become hours, hours become days, days become months then years. Before one can stop the damage from being done, it's too late. The damage is done.

She'll walk with less pep in her step, less enthusiasm, less vibrancy, less energy. Basically, less than what she is.

So, women who often have attitudes, or what seem like chips on their petite shoulders, stem from nothing more than disappointment and a lack of satisfaction in not being able to completely set her Inner Sex Goddess free.

There are also those women who have had a taste of Orgasmland. And although their Inner Sex Goddess was not set free, they are very well aware of the pleasure involved in the attempt. This is always good, but some women, due to strict upbringings, always feel ashamed or guilty for experiencing such a pleasure.

These types usually walk rigidly, stiff almost, something holds them back. They can't completely let it go even though the intention is there to be set free.

These women can be a hassle, but if you're willing to invest time, they can be what you create of them sexually. They can become projects that you mold and sculpt to create the perfect liberated Sex Goddess.

Once a Goddess has been freed, it becomes a rebirth of sorts starting from the inside out. Her entire energy will change as well as her personality. She will possess a glow that wasn't apparent before. A glow that now cannot be ignored.

There is not much one can tell from a woman who is catty or talkative in regards to her sexual temperament. Talk can easily be used for reasons other than what the words mean, but a woman who is very verbal will also be verbal during sex.

This is a good thing. You'll get instant feedback on your strokes. And when she chirps the loudest that's when you know you've "struck a chord" so to speak.

A woman speaks to connect and share information. She could be doing this in your presence. If you notice that her baseline behavior isn't very talkative, but suddenly becomes chatty in your presence, she may be excited and/or nervous. She's trying to stand out to you. This displays the effect you have on her. Your work will be effortless.

A woman who wears make-up is doing so for two reasons: 1) because it will make her stand out to men and 2) because men will find her more attractive. The fact that make-up makes her feel good is the result of being found attractive by men.

Do not believe anything otherwise contrary to this. Remember, human biology is not rocket science. It's all quite simple. All the signs are there for us. We just have to open our eyes.

Studies have shown a man and woman who are perfect strangers to each other will develop romantic feelings for one another after holding prolonged eye-contact with each other. Who would have thought?

Our Olfactory System, our good ole' sense of smell, has always played a significant role in human sexuality. It used to be the way people judged people and their level of attractiveness.

If their scent aroused us, we found them attractive and sex ensued. If we did not like the scent, they were banished. Even today, we naturally like the scent of someone we like and dislike the scent of someone we don't like.

With perfumes and colognes, we don't have to rely much on our natural scents to arouse the opposite sex. Women wear perfume to stand out in a bold way, and natural or not, it still has the power to arouse the men who inhale it. So, a woman does not wear perfume with the intention of not receiving attention and arousing men. This is the main reason they wear it.

A woman's hair and how she decides to wear it can only tell you about her personality. Generally, women like to wear their hair down. A lustrous mane displays general health and fertility. And it displays her femininity which makes her hair very important to her.

Although her hair is important, a woman who has recently gone through a break-up, a woman who is no longer on the market, or a woman who is starting over in her life will often go to the extreme and cut off most of her hair.

Women don't do this just because. There is always an underlying emotional reason. If she decides to keep her hair short, then it is because this is the look that fits her personality. The initial chopping of the locks though is something far deeper.

Taking everything into account, a woman who has long flowing hair, has eye-makeup and lipstick on, who wears perfume and who moves with authority is one you can guarantee is very healthy sexually.

A woman who is very healthy sexually can be pinpointed just by doing a casual once over. Her energy will glow, her skin will be radiant, her eyes will sparkle and she will generally be happy and care-free.

When her sexual needs have been met, all other problems seem to disappear. They just roll off like a bead of sweat. When a woman's sexuality prospers, her over-all health prospers because it is meant for her to be happy sexually. It is in her nature. This is just the way it is for our females.

A woman's clothes do well to hide and/or reveal the flesh of a woman, but they do not yield an accurate assessment of her sexuality. Clothes can be worn to achieve a certain effect.

For instance, a shy woman may wear something revealing just to receive attention. She may want to be seen as a sexual being although it's not really who she is (yet). Or a woman may cover-up her body just to be seen as wholesome and pure although she really isn't. Therefore, the clothes do not render anything accurate.

The absolute truth of the matter is a woman would rather be comfortable, warm and secure. Basically, she would rather be naked and caressed by soft sheets and comforters than walk around with clothes on. A woman is at her sexiest when she is naked because she is in her most natural state.

Sure, clothes do a great job in revealing what needs to be seen, what doesn't need to be seen, what need to be hinted at and what needs to be emphasized or minimized. They even help to entice, flirt and attract the opposite sex.

Just because clothes do all of these things for women, does not mean women don't want you to rip them off their bodies. Clothes are worn for her to suggest what lies underneath.

A woman who plays coy is still begging deep down

to be rid of her clothes. A woman who wears a low cut top revealing glorious amounts of cleavage is aware of how easily her breasts can be accessed.

And women who wear dresses and/or skirts are very well aware of how easily their naughty parts can be reached for sex.

Keep these things in mind when you spot a woman with a low-cut top and/or short skirt. She does not wear these articles by accident. She wears them because they make her attractive to a man which in turn makes her feel sexy. Observe and the world shall reveal itself to you.

WOMEN THROUGH THE AGES

From the time a woman reaches sexual maturity to the time she's matured well into her golden years, a woman will progress through various stages of her sexuality. This is a journey, not only of self-discovery, but of trying to unleash and keep alive her Inner Sex Goddess. A woman's overall heath depends on it.

The full extent of a woman's sexuality cannot be fully realized until her Inner Sex Goddess has been released but this cannot happen until she has been found and so we have the beginning.

When a young woman becomes sexually active, around mid-teens, she is in a state of hormonal imbalance. She's at the state of emergence, revealing to the world that she is a young woman. It is during this time that she is discovering what she likes and dislikes.

However, because of the raging hormones, her

critique of sex takes a back seat to the actual deed itself. The deed becomes most important. How good or how bad the deed was becomes secondary. At this point, her Inner Sex Goddess has yet to be found.

In her early twenties to about twenty-five, the hormonal imbalance has finally balanced itself out. Now the deed itself, although still important, shares the stage with performance.

It is during these years a young woman begins to experiment with different settings, people, and moods. She tries on different kinds of sex to see what she likes best. By her mid to late twenties, she will know exactly what she likes and will do her best to get it. It is usually in a woman's twenties that she will find her Inner Sex Goddess. She will have found through it orgasm but still not released her.

It is in a woman's thirties that she will typically reach her sexual peak. This is usually where she is able to have her Inner Sex Goddess unleashed. Any qualms she may have had in her twenties concerning sex cease to exist when a woman hits her thirties.

Now, she not only know what she likes and how to get it, but she is confident and in complete control of her pleasure. She knows that as long as she is taken care of sexually, everything else will be taken care of.

The thirties also mark a trying time for women. They feel they aren't that young anymore and therefore not as attractive as they once were. They feel they can't compete with women in their twenties. The frequency in which she's "picked up" or "hit on" by men begins to diminish. She may feel like she is no longer in the running.

Through all this though, her Inner Sex Goddess is still afloat. She hasn't gone anywhere. But the woman may become frustrated at men who can't see her for the Goddess that she is. And so she will put out subtle cues meant only for those rare men who are aware thus weeding out those who would be a complete waste of her time.

This is where her communication begins to take on a deeper hidden sexual tone. Since she is frustrated and not being taken to Orgasmland, she'll speak of her sexual frustrations verbally, but not in words so clear.

She'll begin to speak an even deeper sub-language, one she is not completely familiar with or well versed in, because before there was no need to speak it. She was satisfied before; now, not so much. She must resort to her natural weapons of language and communication to voice what she cannot come right out and say.

Beginning in her late thirties to about the age of forty-five, a woman will become very well versed in saying what she needs sexually. Saying it and not saying it. This is also the time where she cuts out all of the child's play from the equation. If you want to have sex with her, it's best to be up front because she doesn't have time for games. Games are for children and have no place with a mature Sex Goddess.

This is the woman who will tell you exactly what she wants and what she's looking for. All you have to do is listen. These women are very fun because you know what to expect of her and she know what to expect of you.

All women would consider having nothing but a sexual relationship, but women in this age bracket are more mature and so know how to deal with it better than the others. Their heart strings won't become involved as easily as a younger woman's would.

Women of this age bracket also won't be offended as easily by your wandering ways or suggestions in introducing something or someone else into your sex play with her.

Women in the late forties well into her fifties know themselves so well that, although they would prefer a man to play with, they don't necessarily need one. She can take care of herself. At this age, she's reached the state where her Inner Sex Goddess is fully free. This woman has no qualms or inhibitions about her sexuality.

She is comfortable in her own skin. She's comfortable with herself, her body and her needs. Women in this age bracket are easy to please because sometimes all they want is a warm masculine body to ravish theirs and that's it. Your deed is done and you'll be on your own merry way. There will be no mistaking your purpose.

These women have long loved and long lost and aren't bright-eyed or naïve as younger women tend to be. They won't fall in love as quickly and are keen to all the tricks of the trade. Respect a woman in her fifties and above. They have been around longer and have seen and done it all.

As a woman moves into the golden years, her temperament is generally the same as those in their fifties, but becomes more frustrated and out of the loop as the choices for sexual partners slowly decreases. This does not mean she has lost her desire for sex or that her Inner Sex Goddess has disappeared. On the contrary, her desire and her Inner Sex Goddess are screaming to be satisfied.

It's just now, it doesn't show as well as it used to. Given the opportunity, women in this age bracket would love to spend the remainder of their lives fulfilling their Inner Sex Goddess. So don't think that the sweet old lady across the street is just a sweet old lady. She was once young. She was once vibrant, and she still has in her that Sex Goddess. Venture close if you dare. You have been warned.

Genghis knew the
Ancient method well.

THE SECRETS OF SILENCE

The saying "Silence is Golden" has more truth to it than one would have you realize. When someone is silent, it strikes a deep rooted nerve in people that make them wonder what's going on. People tend to be reaction seeking. They need a certain stimulus. They expect you to react to them the way they do you.

Silence curbs this vicious cycle and puts you in a position of power. Some things don't require a verbal answer. There is a reason they say "he's the strong silent type" and not "he's a strong talkative type."

Silence is one of the Seducer's most powerful weapons. This must not be over-looked or forgotten. You must keep this at the forefront of your mind. Sometimes it is what is not said that carries the most weight. In matters of Seduction and dealing with women, silence can be used to get where you want to be with her.

Most men tend to believe that they must be chatty

and "talk up" a woman in order to succeed sexually with her. Nothing can be further from the truth. Talking a woman up places you in the friend zone at the start and from there you hope to finish in her bed. The reason most men use this method is because it is the only one they know.

They were never taught the true right of man. It only takes a few choice words to find out everything you need to know about a woman. Anything other than that and you are digging yourself into a hole that will be hard to climb out of.

The silence you use in between your words says a lot about your character. It shows that you are not reaction seeking nor shaky in her presence; that you're not in a hurry or full of goofy energy. That you are not hanging on every word or smiling, it displays to her that you are confident and comfortable, both in yourself and with her.

After she's finished speaking, let silence linger in the air for a bit before responding if you respond at all. This creates sexual tension and changes the mood and the atmosphere into one more sensual between you and her.

By having her within your presence and having used silence to your benefit, she will long to return to such an atmosphere. The looks you give her, the silence you employ, the tension in the air all make for a ripe Seduction.

Perhaps you have heard of the "awkward silence" people usually encounter when getting to know each other. This usually happens when a man and a woman are engaged in conversation and suddenly both parties stop talking. The silence they experience is not at all "awkward." It is just uncomfortable for them because they don't know how to deal with such a silence.

SOLOMON'S WAY

That silence was not by accident and not misplaced at all. That silence was there to not only to create sexual tension, but it was also placed there so the man would shut up already and kiss her.

Yes, it is true. If a man is too dumb to know how to use silence, women will use it themselves hoping you get the picture and do what you're supposed to do. The silence helps create the mood and once it's there, it is your job to act on it.

This does not mean trying to think of something to say in order to fill the silence. This means actually doing something, like going in for the kiss or taking her hand or something to that effect. This demonstrates that you are confident with the silence and you know exactly what to do with it. A woman who is excited, nervous or not yet comfortable with silence will quickly try to fill the void with words of her own. This is okay. Just let her talk and when she's done, deploy the silence.

Silence creates uneasiness in women because they think you can hear the thoughts running around in their heads. Not just any thoughts, though. The dirty ones. The dirtiest of thoughts. When you use silence with a strong look in the eyes, she'll not only think that you can hear her thoughts but you can also read them on the other side of her eyes.

Of course this is amusing, but no laughing matter. She should feel your desire for her in the air, in your presence, in your eyes and in your silence. She'll be putty in your hands.

It is for this reason that Seducers do not talk as much as the next man. He limits his worth and his impact on the fairer sex if he does so.

A Seducer chooses his words carefully. Then, he structures them, composes them in a way to suggest and insinuate at something delightful. He never just rambles at the mouth. This is what women do and not what they expect men to do.

The power of silence can be used in something as an introduction. Simply introduce yourself, ask the woman how she is and remain silent. She'll tell you everything you need to know. There is no need to try to connect on every little thing she says unless you want to be her friend.

You don't need to find common ground with her. The fact that she is a woman and you are a man is common ground enough. Everything else is just background noise. Of course, this does not mean you do not answer her when she asks you a question. You answer, keeping it brief and turn the spotlight back on her. Remember, it's not about you. It is always about her. She does not care how awesome you think you are. Only how awesome you think she is.

Every encounter does not need to be one in which you or she speaks. The silence between you can speak volumes that would otherwise be ruined by words if you were to speak. There is great understanding and great comfort in silence when both of you can sit together, not saying a word.

The power of silence shall not be left unrecognized or used in the fulfillment of your desires or the completion of your endeavors. It is a very powerful tool in the arsenal of the Seducer.

SOLOMON'S WAY

A true Seducer is
able to recognize and read
what a woman
says with her eyes.

H.I.S. - HER INNER SEX GODDESS UNLEASHED

From the time a young woman becomes aware of her sexuality, she is trying to find, set free and keep satisfied a part of her that beckons to be released: Her Inner Sex Goddess.

A woman's Inner Sex Goddess is that part of her sexuality that is her sexuality. She has a life of her own that is sexually adventurous, sexually uninhibited, and sexually confident and the one who lives in the world of orgasm. Orgasmland is her home and she is the link that connects every woman to this wonderful place. Her Inner Sex Goddess is connected to everything sexual within a woman. Everything. A touch here or there, sexually stimulates HerInner Sex Goddess, but does not truly find her.

Her Inner Sex Goddess requires more than simple sexual intercourse to be discovered and even more to be unleashed. With every moan and every thrust, Her

Inner Sex Goddess comes closer to being found. It is not until after a woman has reached orgasm and can continue to reach orgasm that Her Inner Sex Goddess has been found.

This is a time of great discovery for the woman. From this moment forth, she will be focused and determined. Her goal, to reach Orgasmland the best way she knows how. She knows that upon finding Her Inner Sex Goddess, it would go against who she is, to leave her bound and restrained. She knows that she must be set free.

Her Inner Sex Goddess must be unleashed. It is only after a woman experiences multiple orgasm can this happen. Not multiple as in three in one day. Multiple as in back to back to back, rapid succession. This launches her into centerfield of Orgasmland at the same time breaking all restraints that held Her Inner Sex Goddess captive.

Underneath the light of many moons, Her Inner Sex Goddess merges with the woman taking complete control of her body from that moment forth.

Soon, the "after glow" from these many moons wears off and she slowly falls back to earth concluding her trip to Orgasmland. But when a woman returns to earth from Orgasmland, she does not leave Her Inner Sex Goddess behind. Quite the contrary. This woman now is Her Inner Sex Goddess

She blends in like a normal ordinary woman, but she is no longer ordinary. Under closer examination, we see that the way she moves is more confident, more fluid. Her skin sparkles and glows. Her eyes speak of a world far removed from earth.

She is a Sex Goddess far away from home here and desires to return home to Orgasmland. Her vision will seek out ways to return there. Her body will move in a way to return there. Her speech will hint at returning there. Any opportunity that suggests even going near Orgasmland will be gladly accepted with open arms and legs.

The Sex Goddess feeds off sex in hopes to return home. But she is not in frenzy. She exhibits a care-free attitude, any and all bitterness that may have been present is now gone. It is with this attitude that she is able to mingle and gossip with fellow Sex Goddesses. The shared joy of orgasms and Orgasmland has the power to bring together Sex Goddesses from all over. They all have a common ground form which to build. The women who have not yet unleashed Her Inner Sex Goddess will usually seek knowledge and wisdom in hopes of doing so soon.

Every woman is born with Her Inner Sex Goddess within her. Sometimes, one session of multiple orgasms is not enough to unleash her. So another session is demanded. It is the job of the Seducer not only to help women find Her Inner Sex Goddess, but also to unleash her.

When a Seducer looks into a woman's eyes, he is not looking at what she is on the surface. No, he is looking deep within her. He is looking at Her Inner Sex Goddess. This is what you shall have surrounding you, Sex Goddesses. They'll praise you because they know you can help them all return home to Orgasmland.

On Earth there exists two worlds, that of Earth and that of Orgasmland. Orgasmland is ruled by the Goddess of Sex which is Venus. Venus is the spirit within every woman on Earth as a Sex Goddess. Women are both human and of the spirit. Most of the time, women endure the human side of life and not the spiritual side. This causes a great imbalance within them. Instinctively, they will try to unleash their Sex Goddess so they can become whole and healthy. It goes against the heart of Venus to have her restrained.

16

THE SECRET LIFE OF A SEDUCER

The life and exploits of a Seducer are not on immediate display for all to see. What he does with his women is between him and his women. A Seducer must use discretion wisely. He must be able to keep secrets in much the same way a woman can keep secrets. And women are masters of keeping secrets.

A Seducer does not boast about his sexual conquests or of his ability to anyone. He does not gain any points, satisfaction or confidence in trying to impress others. He possesses all of these things already, naturally.

The only opinions that should matter to him, if any at all, are those of the women he seduces. The reason they would matter, even a little, is because they are the ones you must please and sometimes it pleases them to feel heard, to have their thoughts and feelings validated. This would be the only reason. He does not care what her opinions are about him. If you are good enough to have sex with her, you are good enough, period.

A Seducer's job is to provide pleasure and protection to women, they understand the inner workings of women in a way no one else can. They analyze them, taking in their essence. They become masters of women through instinct and through practice, the become gods of their craft.

There are no tricks, no lies, no smoke screens that a Seducer must employ to achieve his ends. That is for the lowly. A true Seducer knows what lurks within all women and completely understands that nonsense is not needed.

As a Seducer, you must be able to see the straight line within all the circles present. You must be able to see through all of the distractions, all of the glitz and glamour, all that would discourage you from your goal or providing sexual pleasure to a woman of your choice.

Society wants you to see women a certain way. Do not be fooled. Society is not who matters. Women are the ones who matter and they would like you to see them for what they really are: restrained Sex Goddesses.

They do not see the world the way men see the world and hate that men seem to think they do. They hate that men are too busy with themselves to care about them sexually. Women are very simple creatures. We men just complicate them.

A Seducer's focus shall never be on himself in her presence. A woman expects you to be strong and confident which means putting the focus on her because that's what she would expect from someone with such traits.

There shall be no guilt or reservations when it comes to your desire for women. It is your duty to fulfill their needs and it is what they want of you. Play not into the hands of those who would tell you your goals are misdirected. You cannot hope that one would understand where you are coming from. They won't. And it is useless trying to convince anyone of anything related to your pursuits. Your energies will then be misdirected.

A Seducer must never lose his footing when dealing with women. This means lashing out in anger or losing your temper. Doing so only shows that you have no self-control and are not in charge of your emotions. Woman may become upset for whatever reason, but under no circumstances shall you make their problems yours.

More often than not, when a woman has a problem, she just wants an ear to listen to her. Not a mouth or a man to solve her problems for her. Unless directly questioned for help, just listen. She'll tell you all you need to know.

A Seducer does not feel guilty or ashamed of his power over women. It is his birthright to be a king. A woman doesn't mind lavishing her king with all she can to make him feel more royal because in her eyes, he is a Sex God. Women will come to your defense in and out of your presence. No harsh words shall be levied your way without her holding up a shield and striking them down with sword of fire that is her wrath.

Women are fierce warriors and are motivated by something far deeper than what the eye can see. Women will keep your kingdom secure, beautiful and free from anything that would oppose you or what you stand for. A man whose purpose in life is to fulfill women will in turn be fulfilled. Doors open more easily when first caressed by the sweet whispers of a woman.

SOLOMON'S WAY

Naysayers and non-believers may work hard to put a crack in a Seducer's armor to no avail. Slight blemishes can easily be buffed out by the loving hands of a fair maiden. A knight, no less, but a king shall emerge victorious over his detractors, and his many queens shall save a laughter for the most indignant. A Seducer does not worry about what others think of him or his envious ways. For if those who oppose him shall be imparted but a glimpse of his expertise, they too shall live worry free.

Wisdom shall be given, but only to those who are deemed worthy. Explosives in the hands of the clumsy can only extinguish any hope of salvation once the fuses are lit. Be kind to those who are not as wise and whose eyes have not been opened. The blame is not their own, but the environment from which they came which did not show them the keys to the locks of the world.

Seducers must stand on the highest mountains and peer deep through the clouds that blind mortal men. They must be able to distinguish mere trees from walking men and women from sirens of the sea.

Eyes that are closed cannot hope to see but the veil that cloaks their sight in darkness.

No landscape is too dense, no weather too frigid for a Seducer to come to the aid of a woman in dire need of pleasure. He would rather fancy himself a suit of barbed-wire than to let her cries fall on deaf ears. With the strength of a thousand men and a force greater than the most turbulent waters, he would break free from the confines of the center of the Earth if it meant he could rescue a damsel in distress. Nothing would stop him from falling from the highest tower if it meant he could cushion her fall at the bottom.

ABOUT THE AUTHOR

Christopher J. Solomon was born and raised a Seducer. Having lived at the base of Mt. Etna in Sicily, Italy and on Chestnut Close in London, England, the ways of the Seducer were revealed to him as if by destiny. He possesses a Genius IQ and currently resides in Texas. His home though is the place where he was born in Irvine, California.

Contact the author at kingovhearts80@yahoo.com

COMING SOON

The Seducer's Bible

Solomon's Way: Seducing Women Who Love Women

Memoirs of a Seducer

www.ingramcontent.com/pod-product-compliance
Lightning Source LLC
Chambersburg PA
CBHW031157020426
42333CB00013B/711